Ukraine

Second Edition

South Huntington Pub. Lib.
145 Pidgeon Hill Rd.
Huntington Sta., N.Y. 11746

Catherine W. Cooper
With additional text by Zoran Pavlović

Series Editor
Charles F. Gritzner
South Dakota State University

CHELSEA HOUSE
PUBLISHERS
An imprint of Infobase Publishing

Frontispiece: Flag of Ukraine

Cover: Vydubytsky Monastery, Kiev, Ukraine

Ukraine, Second Edition

Copyright © 2007 by Infobase Publishing

Chelsea House
An imprint of Infobase Publishing
132 West 31st Street
New York NY 10001

Library of Congress Cataloging-in-Publication Data

Cooper, Catherine W.
   Ukraine / Catherine W. Cooper ; with additional text by Zoran Pavlovic. — 2nd ed.
      p. cm. — (Modern world nations)
   Includes bibliographical references and index.
   ISBN 0-7910-9207-0 (hardcover)
   1. Ukraine—Juvenile literature. I. Title. II. Series.
   DK508.515.C66 2006
   947.7—dc22   2006015643

Chelsea House books are available at special discounts when purchased in bulk quantities for businesses, associations, institutions, or sales promotions. Please call our Special Sales Department in New York at (212) 967-8800 or (800) 322-8755.

You can find Chelsea House on the World Wide Web at http://www.chelseahouse.com

Series and cover design by Takeshi Takahashi

Printed in the United States of America

Bang Hermitage 10 9 8 7 6 5 4 3 2 1

This book is printed on acid-free paper.

All links, Web addresses, and Internet search terms were checked and verified to be correct at the time of publication. Because of the dynamic nature of the Web, some addresses and links may have changed since publication and may no longer be valid.

Table of Contents

Ukraine

Second Edition

1

Introducing Ukraine

E urope's second-largest country (after Russia), Ukraine lies in the center of the continent. The country is midway between the Atlantic Ocean to the west and Russia's Ural Mountains to the east. Romania, Moldova, Hungary, Slovakia, and Poland are on its western border; Belarus and Russia are to its north; and Russia is also its neighbor on the east. The country lies north of the Sea of Azov and the Black Sea.

As a result of this "crossroads" location, Ukraine has been influenced through time by many cultures. From the south came the Greeks and Ottoman Turks, who were busily trading and colonizing across the Black Sea; from the north and west came various European influences, including those from Poland, Lithuania, and Scandinavia; and from the north and east, Russia cast its long and often ominous shadow. The country's architecture, spoken languages, and the ways of making a living are just some of the cultural traits that have been introduced by outside peoples.

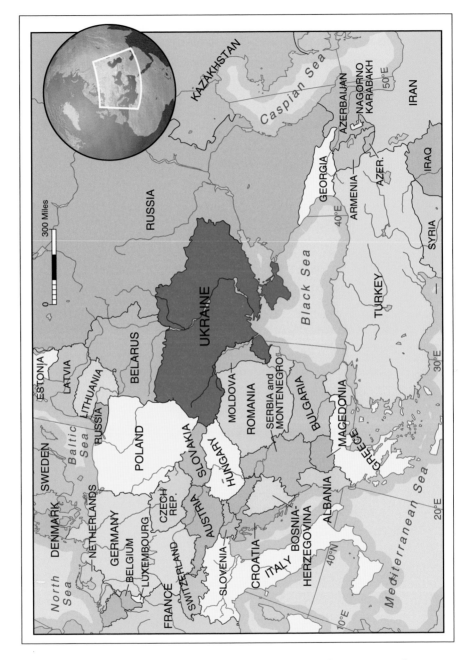

Ukraine is located in eastern Europe and shares borders with seven countries: Russia, the former Soviet Republic of Belarus, Poland, Slovakia, Hungary, Romania, and Moldova. Itself a former Soviet republic, Ukraine is Europe's second-largest country and is nearly the size of the state of Texas.

A study of the physical geography of Ukraine reveals how its natural landscape has been an important factor in the country's historical development. Physical features such as its rich soils and mineral resources have played a major role in Ukraine's economic development. Ukraine's varied landscapes also have attracted different people and cultures who, in turn, have influenced the country's cultural and political development and landscapes. These elements of unity and diversity, of stability and challenge, will guide the way to what lies ahead for this nation of nearly 50 million people in a rich, yet vulnerable part of today's world.

Is Ukraine a borderland or heartland? While the word *Ukraine* in fact means "borderland," the country has, during the course of its history, been both on the fringe and in the heart of regional political and cultural activity. After the middle of the fourteenth century, others in whole or in part controlled the region of eastern Europe known as Ukraine. Yet, in declaring its independence from the Soviet Union in 1991, Ukraine set a course for statehood for which there was little precedent. The country always has had a strong regional identity and, from time to time, fierce independence movements have arisen within the country's borders.

As a part of the extensive Grand Principality of Lithuania in the fourteenth century, then of Poland, the Russian Empire, and the Soviet Union, Ukraine was indeed a borderland, or an outlying region. From time to time, however, the people of much of present-day Ukraine lived under a common government. Ukraine's early history is marked by periods of cohesion—under the Scythians in the seventh to third centuries B.C. and under Cossack horsemen-warriors in the sixteenth through eighteenth centuries A.D. All of these groups left their imprint on the landscape and culture of Ukraine.

The country's national borders are firmly established and respected by agreements with neighboring countries. Building a viable nation, however, requires many other elements.

Establishing a healthy economy and stable political institutions present major challenges to Ukrainians today.

Ukraine and its people suffered greatly in the two World Wars of the twentieth century and during the period of Soviet control. The legacy of Soviet-controlled industry includes outdated power plants that continue to pollute the air and create other environmental problems. The resulting radioactive fallout from the disastrous 1986 nuclear accident at a power plant in the Ukrainian town of Chernobyl still pollutes waterways and the soil. This affects human health, because cows that eat grass grown on contaminated soil may produce milk that can make the people who drink it sick. As Ukraine builds a modern industry and economy, its people are also addressing these environmental issues.

Fortunately, the soil found throughout much of Ukraine is among the world's most fertile. Thus, Ukraine has long been known for the abundance and variety of its agricultural products. Under uncultivated conditions, the vast plains and gently rolling hills have a natural cover of grasses. The *steppes* (drier areas covered with short grasses), *prairies* (covered with taller grasses common to areas with more abundant precipitation), and forested areas of the country enhance its beauty. People enjoy hiking and skiing on the mountain trails, and sunbathing and swimming at Black Sea beaches.

Since declaring independence from the Soviet Union in 1991, Ukrainians have worked to establish a feeling of unity and "nationhood." One of the first concerns has been distinguishing its language from that of Russia's. The Ukrainian form of Cyrillic writing style differs somewhat from the Russian form and employs a slightly different alphabet. This is reflected in the translation of words into other languages, such as English. For example, when the Ukrainian alphabet is used as the basis for spelling an English word, the spelling is different than when the English word is based on the Russian alphabet. Currently, the most common and familiar spellings used for

Thanks to its fertile soil, Ukraine has earned a reputation as being the "breadbasket of Europe." When it was under Soviet control, Ukraine was responsible for more than one-fourth of the Soviet Union's agricultural output. Pictured here is a rose farm in Sokolinoye, on the Crimean Peninsula.

Ukrainian place names are based on the Russian alphabet ("Kiev," for example). But as Ukrainian-based writing becomes more widely recognized, some of the place names will be written differently in English; these "new" spellings (such as "Kyiv" for "Kiev") are shown in parentheses in this book.

Ukraine is a beautiful place with rich natural resources, and its people are known for their strong sense of unity. The citizens of Ukraine now have an opportunity to build a prosperous nation. Understanding the country's physical and human geography is an important step toward gaining an appreciation of its people, the pride they have in their land, and the challenges they face today.

2

Physical Landscapes

Ukraine's physical geography—its natural landscape—is a very important element in helping to shape the country's history, culture, and demographics. The country's rich and varied natural environment has provided humans with many options. Through time, different groups have culturally adapted to, used, and modified the lands in which they have lived. Further, the competing themes of "borderland" and "heartland" have characterized the country's history for centuries.

LOCATION

Ukraine is one of the westernmost countries to emerge from the Union of Soviet Socialist Republics (USSR). It shares an extensive border with Russia and the Black Sea. In absolute location, Ukraine extends from 44° 29' north latitude at Yalta on the south coast of the Crimean Peninsula, northward to approximately 52° 20' north latitude.

If placed over North America, its position would stretch from roughly Minneapolis, Minnesota, to Saskatoon, Saskatchewan. Its farthest western extent is adjacent to Slovakia at about 22° 18' east longitude. In the east, it extends to approximately 42° east longitude.

Ukraine is one of Europe's newest countries and also one of its largest. When it broke from the Soviet Union in 1991, it retained the borders it had as a Soviet Socialist Republic within the USSR. As an independent country, it is second only to Russia in size among European nations. Ukraine has an area of 233,094 square miles (603,700 square kilometers). This is about the size of Arizona and New Mexico combined, or a little smaller than Texas.

The capital city, Kiev (Kyiv), is also the country's largest. The huge urban center is located in the north-central part of the country, at 50° 27' north latitude. This places the city farther north than any part of the United States except Alaska, and at approximately the same parallel as the Canadian city of Winnipeg, Manitoba. At this latitude, Kiev's winter days are short. Around December 21, the sun rises at approximately 8:00 A.M. and sets at approximately 4:00 P.M., providing only about eight hours of sunlight. In late June, on the other hand, Kiev's residents enjoy approximately 16 hours of sunlight per day.

The entire area of Ukraine falls in the same time zone, which is two hours ahead of Greenwich Mean Time (GMT). So, when it is noon in Greenwich (London), England, it is 2:00 P.M. in Ukraine. This difference in time zones illustrates an important relationship between time and longitude. The earth is 360° in circumference. It rotates once every 24 hours, so each hour corresponds to a difference in longitude of 15° (360°/24 hours = 15°/1 hour). Thus, Philadelphia, Pennsylvania, at 75° west longitude, is five hours *behind* GMT (0° longitude) and seven hours behind Kiev time (30° east longitude). When it is 2:00 P.M. in Kiev and noon in London, it is 7:00 A.M. in Philadelphia.

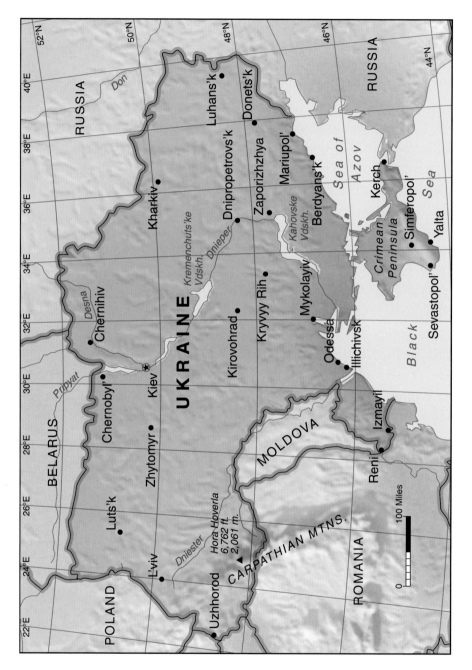

Much of Ukraine is flat; its terrain is primarily made up of fertile plains (steppes) and plateaus. Its highest peak, Hora Hoverla (6,762 feet, 2,061 meters), is located in the Carpathian Mountains, in the southwestern part of the country.

NATURAL LANDSCAPE

Much of the Ukrainian natural landscape is composed of relatively flat lowlands without significant physical, and therefore human, barriers. As a rule, flatlands are more inviting to the formation of permanent settlements than are rugged lands. It is much easier to farm on a plains surface. Relatively flat terrain also offers many advantages in terms of the ease and cost of constructing buildings, highways, and railroads. Plains also provide an "open door" to migrating groups and the resulting cultural diffusion (the flow of ideas and materials). The importance of plains is evident in that nearly all East European capitals are located on relative flat lowlands. Throughout history, the plains of eastern Europe have served as a corridor for migrations between Asia and Europe. Each of the numerous migrating peoples has left racial, ethnic, and cultural marks of their presence. On the other hand, higher elevations and mountains provide refuge areas. In the late 1940s, for example, Ukrainians used the country's mountainous region for protection as they resisted the Soviet military.

Vegetation

The grasslands of Ukraine and western Russia are known as steppes (pronounced "steps"). The natural vegetation is relatively short grass, or a mixture of grass and shrubs. In this semi-arid region, the grasses are shorter and less dense than those on prairie land. Toward the north and west, the short grasslands give way to the taller grasses of prairies. Both the steppes and prairies are located on flat to gently rolling plains. In many respects, Ukraine's natural vegetation landscapes are very similar to those of North America's interior.

On the interior plains of the United States, tall grass prairies gradually gives way to short grass steppes the farther westward one progresses toward the Rocky Mountains. This is one factor that attracted many settlers from eastern Europe's grassland regions to the interior plains of the United States and Canada.

Many of America's early settlers were familiar with woodlands. But those whose culture was preadapted to grasslands—that is, they had already learned how to make grasslands economically productive—were often the most successful nineteenth- and early-twentieth-century settlers of North America's grassland regions. Culture, after all, is humankind's adaptive mechanism. We use physical environment to serve our needs. Thus, even when humans migrate from place to place they prefer environments in which they are already comfortable and able to implement familiar agricultural and other economic practices.

The rich steppe soil supports wildflowers in abundance: poppies, sunflowers, daisies, lilacs, and others. Flowers are cultivated for nectar and are important for honey production. In the northern and western regions of the country, the prairie gives way to mixed broadleaf forests, with trees such as oak, elm, beech, and maple, as well as coniferous forests of pine. More than one-third of Ukraine's original forests have been cleared for agricultural production. Currently, the forest-prairie region covers approximately one-third of the country.

Water Features

Ukraine has approximately 3,000 rivers, many of which flow southward across the country to the Black Sea. For thousands of years, the rivers have brought silt from upstream and deposited it when the streams reached the flat lowlands. These deposits of alluvium (water-deposited silt), in combination with rich grassland sod, have created some of the most fertile soils in the world. In addition, the waterways served as easy transportation corridors from the Baltic Sea to the Black Sea. This route attracted the Vikings from the north to Ukraine, where they settled in the ninth century A.D. The story of these Vikings, what brought them to the region, and what became of them is told in the next chapter.

The Dnieper (Dnipro) River flows southward from Russia through Belarus and enters Ukraine near Chernobyl (Chornobyl').

Over the centuries, the Dnieper River has been the central traffic corridor through the heart of the Ukrainian region. It also has been the dividing line often used to partition Ukraine among the spheres of influence of neighboring states. So the Dnieper has been crucial to defining Ukraine as heartland or borderland, core or periphery. Boundaries between continents—particularly between Europe and Asia—are made arbitrarily. Where appropriate, prominent physical features are used to determine such boundaries, yet on the plains of eastern Europe that was always a difficult task. In times past, the Dnieper River formed a part of the boundary between Asia and Europe. Depending on historical circumstances, this boundary would move east or west from this river. Today, there is general agreement that this boundary follows the crest of the Ural Mountains.

The city of Kiev lies on the Dnieper. Below Kiev, the river flows southeast, makes a turn of about 90 degrees to flow southwest, and empties into the Black Sea. Three huge dams have altered the Dnieper's natural flow and formed reservoirs in Ukraine; they contain power plants that provide hydroelectric energy. Ukraine's second-most important river, the Dniester (Dnister), is located in the far southwestern corner of the country. It flows from headwaters rising in the nearby Carpathian Mountains, and forms part of the country's border with Moldova.

The coastal waters of the Black Sea and the Sea of Azov form Ukraine's southern border. This border is approximately 1,800 miles (2,900 kilometers) long and includes the coast of Crimea, a peninsula that extends into the Black Sea. An arm of the Black Sea reaches through the Kerch Strait, a narrow water passage separating Ukraine and Russia, and forms the Sea of Azov. This sea is actually just a shallow gulf of the Black Sea, a product of ice thawing after the latest ice age, or period of continental glaciation.

During the Pleistocene geologic period (1,800,000 to 10,000 years ago), the Black Sea covered a much smaller area.

Some scientists believe that the then dry basin was home to people practicing early agriculture and enjoying a way of life far advanced for its time. Once ice sheets began to retreat, the water melt caused global sea levels to rise as much as 400 feet (120 meters). Rising water from the Mediterranean Sea reached a level at which it began spilling through the narrow strait that today separates the Mediterranean and Black seas. Torrents of water cascaded into the lowland, rapidly filling the Black Sea basin, and flooding all evidence of the pre-existing civilization that inhabited the land.

Some scholars believe it was this event that triggered flooding of settlements that thousands of years later was recorded in history as the famous flood described in the Book of Genesis and elsewhere in the Bible. Recently, marine archaeologists have discovered the remnants of early settlements on the floor of the Black Sea that once were thriving communities.

The Black Sea has had a profound influence on Ukrainian history and culture. It is both a barrier separating neighbors and a route facilitating trade and communication. The early people who sailed on its waters were intimidated by its sudden violent storms. This may be the reason why Greeks and later Turks called it the "Black" Sea. This is but one of several theories that attempt to explain the name origin.

The Black Sea and the Sea of Azov have a water surface of 178,000 square miles (164,000 square kilometers). The maximum depth of the Black Sea is more than 7,250 feet (2,210 meters). Because of the many rivers depositing freshwater in the sea, its upper layers of water are only about half as saline as that of the ocean.

Another unusual natural feature of the Black Sea is its "dead zone," which lies about 250 feet (76 meters) below the surface. Above the dead zone is an upper layer rich with sturgeon, mackerel, anchovy, and other varieties of sea life. In the dead zone below, however, there is no dissolved oxygen and marine life is unable to live. Some scientists believe that the dead zone can be attributed to a high level of hydrogen sulfide, but the cause remains a mystery.

Unfortunately, since the late twentieth century, the rich upper layer of the Black Sea has also become somewhat depleted. Human-caused pollution is taking a heavy toll on the once abundant aquatic life. Human and industrial wastes, as well as agricultural chemicals—applied to the cropland and washed into waterways—pollute the rivers that flow to the Black Sea. The Black Sea also influences the climate of southern Ukraine. A narrow band of land located close to the sea enjoys milder winters because of the sea's warming capacity. During the summer months, westerly winds transport moisture-laden air that comes from the Black Sea's surface. This moisture results in higher precipitation occurring in coastal areas than in the country's interior. For this reason, Ukraine's coastal region has attracted settlers since ancient times. Greek colonies began to appear in the Black Sea region as early as the seventh and sixth centuries B.C.

Along the southwestern edge of Ukraine's Black Sea coastline lies the large port city of Odessa (Odesa). Farther west and south along the coast, near the country's border with Romania, is a portion of the Danube River delta. (Most of the delta is in Romania.) This important river makes a 1,776-mile (2,860-kilometer) journey across central and eastern Europe. Where it reaches the Black Sea, its delta spreads out to form an extensive low wetland marsh area. The Danube plays a very important economic role for Ukraine. With the opening of the Rhine-Mein-Danube Canal in 1992, Ukraine became linked to western Europe by water without plying the world's seas.

There are other areas of wetlands in the country. Particularly notable are those located along much of the course of the Dnieper River and the famous Pripet Marshes in the north. This huge wetland is Europe's largest marsh; it extends across Ukraine's northern border into neighboring Belarus. Portions of the Pripet Marshes have been drained and cleared.

Landforms

Land features in Ukraine are often described as being "boring." The average elevation is only 574 feet (175 meters) above sea level, about the same elevation as the highest point in Louisiana. Only in the western areas does the elevation rise. South and west of Kiev is an uplands area broken by river valleys, some with canyons as deep as 1,000 feet (305 meters). Only about 5 percent of the country is mountainous: the Crimean Mountains located on the peninsula of the same name, and a short stretch of the Carpathian Mountains in the southwest. The Carpathians form an arc through the Czech Republic, northern Slovakia, southern Poland, Ukraine, and Romania. The highest point in Ukraine is Hora Hoverla, which rises to 6,762 feet (2,061 meters) in the Carpathians. In comparison, the highest peak in the Appalachian Mountains of the eastern United States is North Carolina's Mount Mitchell at 6,684 feet (2,037 meters).

The Crimean Mountains, which rise to over 5,000 feet (1,524 meters), are separated from the coast by a strip of land typically 5 to 8 miles wide (8 to 13 kilometers). The town of Yalta, the port of Sevastopol, and a series of resort communities are located on this coast. The Crimean Peninsula occupies a geographically strategic location. Its importance has been recognized by many who, over the centuries, have attempted to control the peninsula. Natural harbors of this kind are rare in this part of the world. Through time, they have attracted Greek colonies, Tatar settlements, and Soviet naval bases.

CLIMATE

The climate of Ukraine is generally described as being temperate mid-latitude. Actually, the country's climate is somewhat varied, with differences resulting primarily from latitude and distance from the moderating influence of the Black Sea. During summer months, a large high-pressure system lies to the west, over the eastern Atlantic Ocean and portions of Europe. Winds blow eastward from the high-pressure field, bringing

The Crimean Mountains, pictured here, are located on the peninsula of the same name in southern Ukraine. These flat-topped limestone mountains run parallel to the coast and, along with the Carpathians, are one of two mountain ranges in Ukraine.

moisture particularly to the western part of Ukraine during this time. During the winter months, a high-pressure system located over Siberia creates easterly winds (winds are named for the direction *from* which they blow). These winter winds generally bring cold air and drier conditions. Depending upon the strength and dominance of particular air masses, Ukraine's weather can vary greatly. This reality was something that came as a harsh surprise to the armies of Napoleon and Hitler when they invaded this part of the world. Northern and northeastern Ukraine, lying closer to Russia, experience a continental climate with cooler summers and rather long, harsh winters. Winter temperatures in December, January, and February are usually below freezing. Summer temperatures, in June, July, and August, range between 60° and 80°F (16° to 27°C).

The southern half of the country enjoys a dry continental, or mid-latitude steppe, climate, which is drier and experiences occasional drought. Heaviest rainfall occurs during the summer months, often falling in strong thundershowers accompanied by lightning and thunder. The Crimean Peninsula is dry with hot summers and mild winters. Much of it receives less than 16 inches (41 centimeters) of precipitation annually.

Along the southern coast of Crimea is a band of Mediterranean climate. This moderate and very pleasant climate is the same type that allows the cultivation of citrus fruits, grapes, vegetables, and other subtropical crops in coastal California and of olives and grapes in Italy, Greece, and some other lands immediately adjacent to the Mediterranean Sea.

Precipitation varies across the country. The Carpathian Mountain region receives the most rainfall, with an average of 50 inches (127 centimeters) per year. The annual rainfall around Kiev averages 24 inches (61 centimeters). (Similar amounts of precipitation occur throughout much of the interior plains of the United States, extending from the Dakotas to central Texas.) Apart from the mountainous area and the southern tip of the Crimean Peninsula, the southern part of Ukraine receives less precipitation than the northern area.

SOIL

As has already been mentioned, Ukraine is blessed with some of the world's most fertile soils—rich black "Chernozems." This thick soil, noted for its high content of humus (organic material), occupies almost two-thirds of the country. It is the foundation of Ukraine's reputation as the "breadbasket of Europe." Agricultural production has been an important part of Ukraine's economy for many centuries.

Chernozem soils are a type of "mollisol," which underlies many of the world's great grassland regions. In addition to the steppes of Ukraine and Russia, other areas of mollisols include the prairies of North America and the pampas of Argentina.

Mollisols are soft, even when they are dry, and they crumble when touched. The grasses have large root systems that quickly decay as compared to the roots of trees. This is because the organic matter from grass roots does not have to work its way down into the soil from the surface as do decaying leaves and tree branches. The resulting humus gives the soil its dark color and is the primary factor contributing to its high fertility.

Vegetation in dry lands such as those in Ukraine typically burn periodically. Fire is an important element in creating vegetation communities. It causes the release of minerals that plants need in order to grow. Fire also tends to kill woody vegetation, including many varieties of trees, resulting in grasses that thrive in the more open and shadeless environment. Many scientists believe that early people, using fire for hunting and many other reasons, were responsible for creating steppe and prairie grasslands including those extending across much of the North American interior, as well as Ukraine and beyond. Today, truly natural grasslands are found in only a few remote locations. For thousands of years, these fragile ecosystems have experienced widespread change through such human activities as farming and grazing.

This combination of natural features—flat land, adequate moisture, and extremely fertile soil—created an environment ideal for growing wheat. Throughout the centuries, several varieties of this important grain were developed in Ukraine. When many Ukrainians settled in North America during the 1800s, they found that their own seed varieties were much better adapted to the prairies than were the varieties of wheat that had come from England and other wetter areas of western Europe.

OTHER NATURAL RESOURCES

Ukraine is fortunate to have substantial deposits of several valuable minerals. Rich deposits of coal and iron ore are located in the far eastern part of the country. The Donets

(Donbas; Donets'k) Basin is world famous for its extensive deposits of high quality coal. Deposits of iron ore abound in the region of Krivoy Rog (Kryvy Rih). Rail connections over the approximately 250 miles between these two areas have helped make them major industrial centers. Ukraine also has uranium, natural gas, and oil resources, but in quantities too small to meet domestic demands. Other mineral deposits include manganese, titanium, bauxite, and salt.

National Parks and Natural Reserves

Ukraine has several large natural reserves. Askaniya-Nova, located in the steppe region, was designated a private reserve in 1875 and became a national park in 1919. (In 1872, Yellowstone was established as the first national park in the United States.) Askaniya-Nova became an approved biosphere reserve under a United Nations Educational, Scientific, and Cultural Organization (UNESCO) program in 1985.

Two other units have been accepted as biosphere reserves—Chernomorskiy (also called the Black Sea Nature Reserve) and Carpathian. The Black Sea Nature Reserve was established in 1927 and includes some portions of the sea itself, protecting the waterfowl that congregate there. The Carpathian Biosphere Reserve protects a beech forest that has never been cut for timber. It is the only such forest left in Europe. The Shasky National Park in the far northwestern part of the country protects a wooded lake district. The Danube Water Meadows protects the region in Ukraine near the mouth of the Danube River.

Wildlife

In its various regions, Ukraine is home to wolves, fox, lynx, martens, deer, and other mammals. The Carpathian wildcat is legally protected. The Crimean Mountains are home to wild pigs and mountain sheep.

The country has more than 350 species of birds. (North America, by comparison, has about 800 species.) Birds of the steppes include buzzards, falcons, and harriers, as well as Demoiselle cranes, and the steppe eagle. The Danube delta area is a rich wetland and home to several species of pelicans. Because the Sea of Azov is shallow and its coast has many inlets, it is attractive to herons, egrets, and other wading birds.

The features of the Ukrainian landscape and the country's natural resources have attracted people through the ages. Much of Ukraine's history is thus the story of how these people have moved across the region and how and where they have settled.

3

Ukraine Through Time

Dominated by neighboring peoples through the ages, certain regions of Ukraine were influenced by different cultures. One of the keys to understanding the country today is to study the historic experiences of the different regions. Historical geography provides an opportunity to look to the past in order to better understand the present. This is particularly true when one attempts to understand how the culture (way of life) of a people came about in a particular location. For instance, communities bordering the Black Sea had commercial connections with traders to the south and with the maritime powers of the Mediterranean Sea. The northern and western forest/steppe region was tied by waterways to Europe and had settled agricultural communities; while waves of horsemen from the east settled in the eastern and central steppe region.

EARLY PEOPLE

Archaeologists believe that the early inhabitants of present-day Ukraine were groups of nomadic tribes roaming across Eurasia. No one is certain when the first permanent settlements appeared there, but with each new study, the date seems earlier and earlier. Groups of nomadic people inhabited the area that is now Ukraine as early as 5000 B.C. The first of these was the Trypillians, who moved across the land in search of better pastures. Prominent among the peoples who followed were the nomadic Scythians, who flourished on the steppes north of the Black Sea from the seventh to the third centuries B.C. The Scythians were fierce warriors and superb horsemen who actively traded with Greek merchants at outposts in the region.

By 500 B.C., the ancient Greeks had colonized all corners of the Mediterranean region. In the Black Sea region, their settlements were expanding rapidly in response to their role as economic middlemen between steppe peoples and the Hellenic world. The relationship between the Greeks and the Scythians is described in the writings of Greek geographer and historian Herodotus, as early as the fifth century B.C. Not all Scythians were nomads, though. Some of them were agricultural settlers living not far from Greek colonies with which they exchanged goods.

The Scythians supplied the Greeks with honey, grain, furs, cattle, and slaves, and received in return wine, textiles, weapons, and art. The finely crafted gold work that has been found in Scythian tombs is of Greek origin and attests to the early trade. Scythian burial mounds have been found on the steppes.

Why the Scythians' population and influence declined in the region is unknown. Perhaps an extended drought depleted their food supply. But, as the Scythians' influence faded, another nomadic people eventually became just as prominent as the Scythians had been in Ukraine.

During this period of history, a series of tribes ruled the East European plains. They would move northward from the

By the fifth century B.C., Greece had established a number of colonies on the Black Sea in what is today southern Ukraine. One such colony was Chersonesus, which is located near present-day Sevastopol, on the Crimean Peninsula. Nicknamed the "Ukrainian Pompeii," Chersonesus was founded in 421 B.C.

Caucasus area or westward from Siberia across the Ural Mountains in order to conquer and pillage. Then, after some time, conquerors would settle down until a new wave of tribal peoples arrived, created confusion and chaos, and yet another chain reaction migration. Present-day Ukraine is an ancestral land of many Germanic and Slavic tribes who later formed most of Europe's nations (the territory occupied by a nationality of peoples).

During the Roman Empire's zenith, westward migration across Europe was successfully controlled. But by the fourth century A.D., what once had been the world's strongest power was in disarray. In the absence of Roman strength, Huns invaded from Asia in the fourth century, triggering further waves of migration that forever changed the geopolitical landscape of Europe. Many groups migrated to other parts of Europe, while the area of present-day Ukraine continued to be filled with newcomers.

In the early Middle Ages, Ukraine's population presented a human ethnic mosaic that included Slavic and Germanic tribes, Avars, Bulgarians, Huns, various Turkish tribes (Finns and Hungarians), and others. Slowly, however, Slavic cultural dominance began to prevail, primarily because Slavs were the largest population group. Conquering groups such as Bulgarians and Avars usually had smaller populations that were easily absorbed into Slavic culture.

According to legend, Kiev was founded during the Slavic expansion in the fifth century. A tribal leader named Kyi (Ky) and his two brothers and a sister picked the site on the bluffs above the Dnieper River, on the west bank (the right bank, as one faces downstream). They believed the location was an ideal site for developing a regional trading center. Because of its location on a bluff overlooking the river, it also could be easily defended.

Another cultural element was introduced into southeastern Ukraine with the arrival of the Khazars, who were of Turkic and Iranian stock and originally from the Caucasus region between the Black and Caspian seas. The Khazars eventually settled in the region during the eighth century, establishing their capital and major trading center near the mouth of the Volga River at Itil. This location, where the Volga flows into the Caspian Sea, was important. Not only were the Khazars able to conduct a prosperous trading operation with the neighboring Slavic people, but they went on to build a huge commercial empire. By settling north of the Caucasus Mountains, the Khazars also effectively blocked Arabs from invading northward and westward into Ukraine and farther into Europe.

By the second half of the eighth century, the Khazars had expanded westward and controlled Ukraine to the Dnieper River. They built towns, engaged in farming, and were actively involved in trade and commerce. In an unusual occurrence, the ruling class of Khazars adopted Judaism in about 740. Rarely has conversion to Judaism happened en masse, and why this happened with the Khazars is not known. While some of the original Khazar settlers were Jewish, the mass conversion was most likely initiated by a headman proclaiming it should be done.

KIEVAN RUS

During the eighth and ninth centuries, Scandinavians known as Vikings ventured far from their northern home, spreading west, east, and south—eventually as far as the region now known as Ukraine. Some raiders settled in England, Ireland, and France, while others sailed farther west to colonize Iceland. The Vikings eventually also traveled across the Atlantic Ocean, settling in Greenland and even reaching—temporarily—North America. Other Norsemen known as Varangians, probably from Sweden, crossed the Baltic Sea and established settlements in what is now Estonia and Latvia. From these small countries facing the Baltic, they continued southward, establishing a fortress and trading center at Novgorod, in present-day Russia.

Over time, they used the waterways, including the mighty Volga River, which linked the Baltic with the Caspian Sea. Once they found and were able to control this vital route, they established commercial links with the eastern Mediterranean. The Varangians also found river links to the Dnieper River and on to the Black Sea. This step ultimately led them to the region's most important trading city at the time—Constantinople, capital of the Eastern Roman Empire (present-day Istanbul, Turkey). There they provided service to emperors as military men and explorers. In terms of contributions to Ukrainian culture, this event was perhaps the most important in their history.

The encounter between Varangians and emperors in Constantinople would lead to further political connections during the following decades. To attract pagan peoples into their political and economic sphere, the Eastern Roman Empire (in much of the literature, known incorrectly as Byzantium) would demand that they become Christians. In order to benefit from the riches of Constantinople, many of the pagans readily agreed to conversion. In this way, the Kievan Rus would eventually become a part of the Christian world. But the relationship was with Constantinople, rather than Rome, hence, they became Eastern Orthodox Christians.

In later centuries, with the rise of territorial aspirations of tsarist Russia and the decline of the Eastern Roman Empire, Russian tsars (pronounced "zar") reminded everyone that it was they who were leaders of Eastern Orthodox Christianity. This meant that Moscow had aspirations to rule the entire Slavic world, which included the Ukrainians. During the twentieth century, much of the region continued to be dominated by Slavic rule based in Moscow.

Scandinavian founders of this state were a small minority. As was previously noted, most conquerors, because their groups were in the minority, almost without exception adopted the local culture within a generation or two. From its beginning, the Kievan Rus was Slavic in nature, with a small group of acculturated (culturally absorbed) Scandinavians forming its ruling elite. In 882, a Scandinavian named Oleg won control of Kiev and established the state of Kievan (Kyivan) Rus. Ukraine, Russia, and Belarus all trace their national history to this eastern Slavic state. Oleg made Kiev his capital and the center of his trading realm. In so doing, Ukraine did indeed become a major "heartland," or an important "core" region. Kievan Rus traders moved along the Dnieper River and along connecting portages south to Byzantium and north to the Baltic. It was a "water road," a "road from the Varangians to the Greeks." In 965, the Kievan warrior-prince Sviatoslav took his forces into the Khazars' territory, crushed their armies, and destroyed their capital, Itil. Thereafter, the Khazars' influence north of the Black Sea declined, and Kievan Rus dominated trade, for a time, on the Volga route. Under a series of strong rulers, Kievan Rus developed trade and commerce, extracted tribute, and influenced a vast territory for the next 350 years.

THE GOLDEN HORDE

Although Kievan Rus never covered all of present-day Ukraine, it exercised more centralized control than had the various bands that lived in the region. With the mid-thirteenth-century conquest by the Mongols, or the "Golden Horde," the large and somewhat cohesive area and peoples of Ukraine began to be pulled in different directions. Mongols under Batu Khan, grandson of Genghis Khan, conquered Kiev in 1240, marking the end of the Kievan Rus period of Ukrainian history. The region became more like a border to other neighboring lands rather than a distinct central core of culture and power. The "borderland" period of Ukraine's history had begun. During this period, the cultural boundary between Europe and Asia shifted westward. At that time, Europe was beginning to exit from the long slumber of medieval stagnation and western Europe was starting to grow in power and political importance. This was the beginning of a period in which eastern lands under Mongol control were considered to be a part of Asia, rather than of Europe. Even today, racist-tainted statements about Russians and Ukrainians being Mongols and Asians are occasionally noted.

Again, different parts of the Ukraine had different experiences. The two principalities of Galicia and Volhynia, in the southwestern region extending along the Dniester River to the Black Sea, retained their Kievan Rus heritage for a time. In Crimea, the Muslims established a "Khanate" and became vassals of the Ottoman Turk empire based in Constantinople. The people of the Crimean Khanate were called Tatars. The Golden Horde held sway over much of the central part of the region as the western province of the vast Mongolian empire was divided into several administrative units.

Ukraine's European neighbor to the northwest, the Grand Principality of Lithuania, grew strong, and Lithuanian princes gradually moved eastward, pushing back the Golden Horde. The people of Ukraine generally welcomed them and were incorporated into the local government. Lithuanian newcomers adopted the local culture, accepting the Orthodox Christian religion and the local language throughout the fourteenth and early fifteenth centuries. But gradually, the Lithuanian influence gave way to Polish dominance in neighboring Ukrainian lands.

During this time, both Galicia and Volhynia had come under the dominance of Poland. In the mid-fourteenth century, a Polish king had set out to control the region, justifying the action, in part, as an effort to extend the Roman Catholic faith over people practicing Orthodoxy. Increasingly, Polish influence made a strong imprint on the people of the region. Most people within the region became Roman Catholic, Latin was adopted as the official language, and the head of the government was Polish. Members of Ukraine's elite population became less interested in local affairs as they identified increasingly with the ruling culture. In the late sixteenth century, a distinctly Ukrainian faith was formed, the Uniate Church. It acknowledged the pope in Rome as leader, but retained Orthodox forms of worship similar to those of the Greek Catholic Church. The new faith reflected the history and different influences at play in the region.

THE COSSACKS

As Polish influence, such as Roman Catholicism and feudal serfdom, became more dominant in the west, those who opposed this influence looked to the sparsely inhabited eastern steppe region called the "wild fields" as a place to settle. For centuries, people had traveled there seasonally to hunt, fish, and gather honey. Now people from Polish-controlled areas in the west began to move eastward to escape the life of the serfs, who were virtually slaves to the owner of the land on which they lived.

These "refugees" from the west joined bands of horsemen called Cossacks, which derives from *kazak*, meaning "adventurer" or "freeman" in Turkish. As peasants also fled Poland and Lithuania to escape serfdom, they were incorporated into Cossack bands, which had already become established on Ukraine's steppes. In addition, Slavic people who sought refuge from attacks by Tatars joined the Cossacks, too. By the mid-sixteenth century, a large community of Cossacks had established themselves in the region. These people practiced a rudimentary form of democracy—they elected their leader, called an "ataman" or "hetman," and many decisions were made through a representative group.

Both Poland and Russia recognized the fighting ability of the Cossacks and commissioned them to do battle with people beyond their borders. Although these two countries tried to control them, the proud Cossacks kept their independence. They fought Turks to the south and east and also provided a buffer protecting Poland against the Tatars (even though they refused to come under Polish domination). In the wars and related violence, many Ukrainian soldiers died; so, too, however, did many clergy, Jews, and Polish landlords and officials. In 1648, the hetman Bohdan Khmelnytsky defeated the Polish armies and arrived in Kiev as a liberator. Polish opposition continued, however, as Khmelnytsky tried to create a Cossack state centered on the steppes east of the Dnieper River. He sought help from the Russian tsar, which was confirmed in 1654 by the Pereyaslav agreement. Although Khmelnytsky sought only foreign aid, Russia used this treaty to begin its long period of increasing control over Ukraine.

The following years were unsettled as rival Cossacks bid for power and Russia and Poland vied for influence. A formal partition of Ukraine between Poland and Muscovy (Russia) occurred in 1667 with the Treaty of Ardrusovo. After that, Poland and Lithuania continued their dominance west of the Dnieper River, increasingly drawing the people there under

In 1648, Cossack leader Bohdan Khmelnytsky defeated Poland and established an independent Cossack principality in Ukraine. Unfortunately, in order to receive foreign aid from Russia, Khmelnytsky was forced to sign a treaty with Tsar Alexis, which ensured that Ukraine had to submit to Russian rule. Pictured here is a monument to Khmelnytsky in front of Saint Michael's Cathedral in Kiev.

European influence. The local nobility identified with their peers in Europe, and the serfs continued to be exploited.

Russian influence increased in the east after 1667. In the late 1700s, the armies of Catherine the Great of Russia eliminated the Cossack military in southern Ukraine. This event dissolved the last vestige of the Hetmanate. Russia moved southward to annex Crimea in 1783. The city of Odessa was rebuilt on the Black Sea coast and grew to become an important seaport and cosmopolitan center. In a series of partitions, Poland gave up control of much of the land west of the Dnieper River to Russia. The far southwest, around Lviv, was annexed to Hapsburg Austria. Ukraine effectively had become a borderland of Russia, although it was a very important outlying region.

THE CRIMEAN WAR AND THE
LATE NINETEENTH CENTURY

Western Europe focused its attention on Ukraine in 1854, when the Crimean War began. The root of the conflict was between Moscow and the Turks over who would speak for the Orthodox Christians in the Muslim Ottoman Empire, which included much of Ukraine. Great Britain and France were concerned about the spreading influence of Russia and supported the Turkish ruler (sultan) in the conflict. Russia's long-standing political desire to secure an all-year seaport on the warm Black Sea was blocked by the Ottoman Empire. In order to change the geopolitical picture of Europe, Russia needed to capture the Black Sea's northern shores. Russia, and later the Soviet Union, always had a geopolitical disadvantage against its main competitors. While Great Britain's, France's, and the United States' navies enjoyed easy access to the global sea, the Russian fleet had few available outlets. In fact, particularly because of its lack of easy access to the ocean, until Peter the Great's reign in the late seventeenth and early eighteenth century, Russia had no navy. Russians and Ukrainians were not seafaring people; rather, they were sons of the steppes and forests.

European powers were interested in limiting the spread of Russia's influence on the southeastern European Orthodox countries of Serbia, Romania, Bulgaria, and Greece. At that time, the Ottoman Empire was known as the "sick man of the Bosporus," meaning it was just a remnant of the once powerful force that was now unable to protect its possessions. In this war, British soldiers arrived via the Black Sea, but landed with inadequate supplies to lay siege to the port of Sevastopol. In the cold, rain, and mud, and with little food, many soldiers died from exposure or hunger, as well as from enemy fire. The British government had learned from newspaper accounts that the wounded were taken to crowded hospitals without blankets, clean bedding, or food they could swallow. At the request of her government, Florence Nightingale, a British nurse, led about 40 nurses to the area. She withstood the anger and opposition of military leaders and doctors. Eventually the nurses were allowed to cook reasonable food for the hospitalized men, clean their wounds, and supply straw mattresses and clean sheets from Nightingale's own funds. The soldiers called her the "Lady with the Lamp." Her actions and dedication gave rise to the beginning of nursing as a highly respected career.

The Crimean War was known also for inspiring the "Charge of the Light Brigade," a work by British poet Alfred, Lord Tennyson. This famous poem memorialized the brave soldiers who followed garbled orders to move against an enemy position that was thought to be so strong the British could not possibly succeed. Ultimately, however, the siege was successful and the Russians withdrew from Sevastopol. The Treaty of Paris, in 1856, brought the conflict to an end.

During this time, other changes were taking place in Ukraine. Serfdom was abolished in 1861 and laborers, freed from bondage to the land, were available for other types of work. Industrial development was encouraged, especially in the Donbas region of eastern Ukraine. A working class of people not engaged in agriculture began to emerge in this increasingly important region. This change, however, was slow and seriously lagged behind developments occurring in western Europe. The Industrial Revolution was transforming European nations, but the Russian Empire was far more traditional, and resisted radical changes. Any rapid rise in middle class and personal independence, they believed, could destroy the existing socioeconomic and political system in which the tsar and his small number of supporters were "haves" and millions of people were "have-nots."

During the nineteenth century, Europe experienced many changes. One of them was expansion of nationalistic feelings among peoples without states (politically governed territories). During the nineteenth century, Europe was a continent of empires. The vast Russian Empire, for example, included many ethnic groups who wanted their own independent states. The tsars, however, feared the nationalist feelings of Ukrainians, and in the middle of the nineteenth century, while the region was under their control, they abolished the Uniate Church. Ministers of the Russian government banned Ukrainian writings at about the same time, and basic education levels declined. A few writers, such as Taras Shevchenko (1814–1861), whose work seemed to promote nationalistic feelings, were exiled.

In the southwestern region of Galicia, people living under the Austro-Hungarian Empire often lacked sufficient land to farm so that they could successfully provide adequate food and other necessities. Between approximately 1880 and 1914, many of these poor, landless people left the region to seek a better life in western Europe or North America. Those who stayed behind increasingly developed a strong consciousness of their distinctive Ukrainian heritage.

WORLD WAR I AND THE INTERWAR YEARS

The First World War broke out in August 1914, shortly after the assassination of Archduke Francis Ferdinand, the presumed successor to Austria-Hungary's emperor Francis Joseph. Russia entered the war on the side of Serbia, which the Habsburg Monarchy and Germany attacked. Soon after, fierce battles between the two sides took place in Ukraine. Each side accused Ukrainians of helping the enemy, resulting in their being treated very harshly by both military forces. Russia's military experienced large losses, which shook the country's confidence and generated political unrest. This unrest was a major contributing factor that resulted in the 1917 Russian Revolution. First, in February, tsarist rule was overthrown and later that year, in October (November according to the Western calendar), Communist forces gained control of the country. Russia immediately withdrew its troops from combat and signed a peace treaty with Germany and the Habsburg Monarchy, losing some of its territory in the west, including Ukraine. At home,

During World War I, Ukraine was caught between allegiance to Russia and the Austro-Hungarian Empire, which controlled parts of what is today western Ukraine. Russia enjoyed great success in Ukraine during the war, launching the Brusilov Offensive in June 1916, which essentially broke the will of the Austro-Hungarian Army. Pictured here are wounded Russian troops arriving in the city of Lviv during the war.

civil war between Communists and royalists began and lasted until 1922, when victorious Bolsheviks (Communists) formed the Soviet Union.

Initially, during the revolutionary period, it appeared that Ukraine would achieve a level of self-determination. A representative governmental body was established in Kiev, and a president was elected. In Galicia, the Western Ukrainian Republic was established and the two governments in the west and the east united briefly in 1919.

Ukraine, however, continued to be a battleground. When World War I ended in 1918, Bolshevik armies continued to fight the so-called White Russians, who supported the tsar and the former Russian Empire. The Polish Army then fought the Red (Bolshevik) Army in western Ukraine. Throughout these conflicts, Ukrainian nationalists fought to gain their own independence as a country.

The military actions deeply scarred Ukraine. Its many parts were annexed to the Habsburg Monarchy's successors, the Czechoslovak Republic and Romania; while Poland incorporated Galicia and several other small territories. The rest of the territory became Soviet Ukraine. In 1922, the Ukrainian Soviet Socialist Republic (SSR) was incorporated into the Communist country of the Union of Soviet Socialist Republics (USSR).

The Soviet government, centered in Moscow, now controlled the Ukrainian economy, including its agricultural production, which had suffered severely during the war; as many as one million Ukrainian people died in a severe famine in 1921–1922. A subsequent brief period of less stringent regulation by Moscow allowed agricultural production to revive. During this period, there was an accompanying growth of Ukrainian institutions with expanded education, publication of Ukrainian books, and promotion of Ukrainian culture.

In the late 1920s, however, Joseph Stalin's economic plan for the USSR forced dramatic and harsh changes. Stalin, who succeeded Vladimir Lenin, envisioned rapid economic development and industrialization of the Soviet Union. From the central government in Moscow, the Soviet leader ordered new mines and factories built in Ukraine. He ordered family farms to be merged into "collectives," with quotas imposed for producing certain quantities of food. Farmers became workers on the new state-owned farms; they received only food from the government in payment for their labor. Those who hesitated to turn their land, livestock, and machinery over to the government were forced to comply. If they resisted, they were persecuted, or deported to remote and frigid Siberia. People who worked on the collectives could not eat what they grew, but had to deliver it to government officials. These strict policies caused yet another devastating famine. It is estimated that during 1932–1933, as many as 7 million people may have starved to death in Ukraine.

WORLD WAR II AND THE POSTWAR SOVIET PERIOD

In September 1939, German military forces invaded Poland and launched World War II. However, Nazi Germany and the Soviet Union signed a pact of territorial exchange in Poland and avoided confrontation. Soviets received territory lost two decades earlier and incorporated it into the Ukraine Soviet Socialist Republic. Two years later, however, Adolf Hitler ordered the invasion of Germany's former ally. The war on Germany's eastern front was fought in the USSR, much of it in Ukraine.

Kiev was besieged for 80 days in 1941 and was again the scene of frantic fighting in 1943. Initially, Ukrainians welcomed the Germans, seeing them as liberators from the Soviets. But this positive perception changed quickly: The Nazis engaged in the mass killing of Jews in Ukraine and forced many people to go to Germany as slave laborers. Ukrainians of all ethnicities suffered tremendously from the atrocities of war. All told, some 20 million people in the Soviet Union lost their lives in World War II, most of whom were in Ukraine and Belarus. The fighting destroyed villages, towns, and cities; industrial plants were leveled; farms, including buildings and agricultural equipment, were destroyed; and transportation facilities, including railroad tracks and trains, highways, port facilities, and airports, were ruined. It is estimated that more than 700 cities and towns were destroyed in whole or in part, including more than 80 percent of Kiev.

Ukraine had a population of approximately 40 million in 1940; approximately 5.3 million died in the war, and another 2.3 million were sent to Germany as slave laborers. Sixty percent of Ukraine's Jews were lost in the Holocaust. More than 40 percent of the economy was destroyed, and 10 million people were left homeless. The Red Army counteroffensive began in 1943, and the Soviets gradually regained what was left of Ukraine. In 1944, Stalin forcefully removed the Tatars from Crimea, deporting almost 200,000 of them to remote and frigid Siberia, declaring that they had helped the Nazis. This was a common practice of Soviet leaders—ethnic cleansing (death or physical removal) of those who opposed the revolution.

In February 1945, the heads of state of the United States, Great Britain, and the Soviet Union met in Crimea. At what history records as the Yalta Conference, U.S. President Franklin Roosevelt, British Prime Minister Winston Churchill, and Joseph Stalin determined how various parts of European territory would be governed by the allies following the defeat of Nazi Germany. At the end of the war, the borders on the western edge of Ukraine were redrawn. Poland was forced to give up Galicia and other territories. These and other lands that had been part of Czechoslovakia and other neighboring countries were returned to Ukraine, and therefore to the USSR.

Those who believed in Ukrainian independence continued fighting after World War II in western Ukraine. These "partisans" threatened Soviet troops and were not totally eliminated until the early 1950s.

Stalin died in 1953, and Nikita Khrushchev became leader of the USSR. Khrushchev had spent his early career in Ukraine. In 1954, on the occasion of the 300th anniversary of the union of Russia and Ukraine, Khrushchev transferred the Crimean Peninsula from the Russian Soviet Federated Socialist Republic to the Ukraine Soviet Socialist Republic. In this act, Khrushchev was using the treaty between Russia and the Cossack Khmelnytsky in 1654 as reason to claim Crimea. Territorial exchanges among Soviet republics were not an unusual practice. One reason they could occur with little disruption was that no one could foresee the dissolution of the Soviet empire as a single country. Therefore, internal territorial exchanges made little political difference as long as everyone resided in the

Soviet Union. Often such decisions were unwise in future geopolitical terms. In the post-Soviet era, many of these ethnically divided territories experienced heated ethnic antagonisms and occasional open conflicts. Crimea, for example, is still predominantly populated by ethnic Russians (as it was when Khrushchev transferred it to Ukraine). For this reason, the potential exists for further ethnic unrest and conflict.

From about 1950 to 1985, Moscow's policies toward Ukraine varied. Sometimes the government exercised strict control and suppressed all things with a nationalistic theme. At other times, officials were tolerant of writers, allowed the Ukrainian language to be taught in schools, and permitted a revival of Ukrainian culture. The economy continued to be centrally controlled from Moscow, however, with established production quotas and no allowance for laws of supply and demand to work in an open economic market.

The Soviets did attempt to develop Ukraine's industry, especially during the 1950s and 1960s in the eastern Donbas region. During the 1970s and 1980s, however, what had been development suffered greatly from Moscow's bureaucratic mismanagement, and industrial output declined. Consumer goods were of very poor quality and continually in short supply.

GLASNOST AND INDEPENDENCE

Beginning in the mid-1980s, Ukrainian nationalistic movements received renewed, and increasingly open, attention. Soviet leader Mikhail Gorbachev initiated economic reforms (*perestroika*) and more openness of discussion and news dissemination (*glasnost*). As a result, the Ukrainian language became the Republic's official tongue and members of the Greek Catholic Church were permitted to return to this peculiarly Ukrainian faith.

Social movements emerged, such as environmentalism in response to the 1986 Chernobyl disaster, as did labor organizations in the mines and plants of Donbas. Communist delegates to Moscow were defeated at the polls, even when they ran unopposed. A political party, Rukh, was established. It advocated democratization and human rights, conditions that were all but nonexistent under Soviet control.

Gorbachev faced increasing nationalistic feelings among the various Soviet republics and tried to institute reforms. Many hard-line Communists opposed these reforms and, in August 1991, tried to oust Gorbachev as head of the Soviet government. The two-day attempted coup d'etat (forceful overthrow of an existing government or leader) failed. That same month, the Ukrainian Parliament took advantage of the emerging Soviet political unrest. It declared its independence from the USSR, subject to a popular vote in December of that year. In the election, 84 percent of Ukrainians voted, and 93 percent of them supported independence. Ukraine now celebrates its Independence Day as a national holiday each year on August 24. Ironically, one historical event accelerated the country's path toward independence. In 1945, Ukraine was already formally recognized as a member of the United Nations, even though it was at that time a part of the Soviet Union. This was the result of the Soviet Union's demand for a more equal position in the United Nations. Thus to counterbalance Western influence in the UN, the Soviet Union promoted membership for Ukraine and Belarus, even though they were both Soviet Socialist Republics.

Ukraine's political turbulence during the twentieth century can be illustrated by what transpired in the city of Lviv during this period of transition. In 1900, Lviv was part of the Habsburg Empire. Then Germany controlled it in 1914 at the beginning of World War I. By 1919, it was the seat of the Western Ukrainian Republic, and for a few weeks in 1920, Bolsheviks ran its government. Lviv was part of Poland from 1921 to 1939, when the Soviets gained control. Nazi Germany invaded and held it from 1941 to 1944, when the Soviets once again governed. Finally, in 1991, Lviv became part of an independent Ukraine.

Ukraine has experienced a long and often tumultuous history. Today, its citizens are self-governing, and they cautiously look ahead to a more stable future. They have set out on the difficult road of transforming Ukraine from borderland to an independent country—a heartland.

CHAPTER

4

People
and Culture

In order to gain a good understanding about a particular place or country, one must learn by building layer upon layer of knowledge. An in-depth country study is a process of accumulating a broad array of knowledge. In this book, for example, following a general introduction, you learned about Ukraine's physical characteristics. An overview of the country's historical geography followed. In this chapter, you will learn about the country's people and their culture. Each of these layers is interrelated in some way with all others. Hence, each set of factors forms an essential building block to the understanding of what follows. Culture, or a people's way of life, includes everything we do as humans. All our actions are products of cultural systems. Population and settlement patterns, types of economic activity, religious practices, and so forth, are products of our culture. Such manifestations vary geographically (spatially) as they result from historical circumstances.

In the early twenty-first century, Ukraine's primary cultural concern has been its declining population.

POPULATION

In 2006, Ukraine's population was estimated to be approximately 46.7 million, almost 2.4 million fewer than in 2000. Ukraine's population reflects a demographic (the statistical study of the human population) pattern similar to that of many former USSR republics. Population growth in the Former Soviet Union during the twentieth century experienced several obstacles. First, atrocities in both World Wars took a terrible toll on human life. Even today, several generations later, women far outnumber men. This is rather interesting considering that East Slavic societies are traditionally patriarchal and having sons is more desirable than having daughters. Communism, however, contributed to another aspect in the decline of the population. It was the emphasis on emancipation and formal education of women that caused a sharp decrease in Ukraine's fertility rates (fertility rates are equal to how many children a woman will give birth to between the ages of 15 and 49), a trend throughout Europe. Finally, transformation of Ukraine from rural agricultural society into modern industrial nation further influenced declining rates of the population growth (urban families generally have much smaller families than do rural families). All these factors have built the foundation for an attitude that smaller is better; therefore, many families are satisfied with having fewer children than previous generations.

After the dissolution of the Soviet Union, Ukraine's harsh economic conditions also contributed to extensive emigration. Some, particularly Ukraine's ethnic Russian population, left for Russia, others migrated to western Europe and North America, and many who stayed behind are still searching for a way out. The result is that Ukraine leads the world in population decline, both in terms of out-migration and also the rate of natural population increase (RNI), which stands at a negative 0.6 percent.

Because of the reasons mentioned above and Ukraine's continuing economic problems, couples are discouraged when they want to raise and support a large family. With an improving economy, the population growth rate may change. The latest available data, however, anticipate a continuing decline in Ukraine's population. It is estimated that the population will drop to about 42 million by the year 2025 and to 33 million by 2050. A declining population places a heavy burden on a welfare state. It also sharply reduces the country's labor force and therefore its potential for economic growth and development. If a country is to grow economically, it must have an adequate workforce. The only option is to import laborers from elsewhere—that is, to open the doors to immigrants. In this traditionally xenophobic (fear of foreigners) part of the world, however, this is the least desirable option for local governments and the citizens themselves. An additional problem, of course, is that even if needed, few people would want to migrate to a country with such a poor economy. Population issues in Ukraine, as well as in many other countries (including the United States) can potentially raise serious political problems.

Another indicator of a country's overall condition of environmental quality and human health and well-being is life expectancy at birth. Currently in Ukraine, overall life expectancy at birth is 70 years, 65 years for men and 76 years for women. These numbers are well below average for the developed world. In the United States, for example, life expectancy is already more than 80 years and in Japan even higher. Various lifestyle aspects contribute to Ukraine's relatively low life-expectancy rates. Difficult economic conditions, lack of advanced health-care services (especially in rural areas), smoking, and a traditional fondness for excessive drinking of strong alcoholic beverages are just some of the factors. The situation appears to be gradually improving, however, and the trend may continue. If economic growth occurs, it will lead to greater prosperity, which, in turn, will contribute to a better quality of life. Unfortunately, it would take a very long period of time—perhaps many decades—for Ukraine to catch up to the quality of life enjoyed in the world's postindustrial societies.

ETHNICITY

In Ukraine as elsewhere, ethnic structure composition most often portrays historical migratory trends. As one of the more developed areas of the former Soviet Union, Ukraine was a magnet attracting a substantial number of workers from other republics, most of whom were of different ethnic backgrounds. Today, one can find among Ukraine's population people representing nearly all ethnic groups found within the former USSR. On the other hand, thousands of Ukrainians immigrated to other republics. Often they were skilled laborers selected by the government to work on the development of the Soviet economy, or were officers in the Red Army. Today, about 78 percent of the population is ethnic Ukrainian and 17 percent Russian. The remaining 5 percent is divided among Belarusians, Moldovans, Crimean Tatars, Bulgarians, Hungarians, Romanians, and Poles, all in nearly equal numbers.

In terms of ethnicity, two major groups dominate Ukraine's population. Ethnic Ukrainians dominate the population of central and western areas of the country, whereas ethnic Russians are the majority in eastern parts of Ukraine. Many Russians living in the country feel much closer to their Russian motherland, however, than they do to Ukraine. This sense of alienation is strengthened by Ukraine's close economic and social ties with Russia. This situation is commonplace throughout many of the former Soviet Socialist Republics. It is important to understand that many ethnic Russians in newly independent countries face an identity crisis. Until 1991, the ethnic Russian population in this part of the world always lived in one Russian (ethnic group) dominated country, the Soviet

In 1944, Soviet leader Joseph Stalin ordered the forced removal of nearly 200,000 Tatar citizens from the Crimean region of Ukraine. To honor those who died during the deportation, some 20,000 Tatars gathered at a memorial rally in Simferopol in 2004 to mark the 60th anniversary of the tragic event. Today, Tatars make up approximately 0.5 percent of the Ukrainian population.

Union. After the former Soviet Socialist Republics gained independence, the ethnic Russians living outside their ethnic homeland suddenly had to choose allegiance to another country, which was not an easy task. Russians in Ukraine often live in an ethnically homogenous environment. Their cultural ties with Russia are so strong that it will take a generation or more to erase this feeling. Meanwhile, they continue to function as an often unwelcome minority in Ukraine.

In certain parts of the country, this distribution varies. In Crimea, 63 percent of the people are of Russian background, and many Russians also live in the industrial cities of eastern Ukraine. A country that is divided ethnically often experiences internal conflicts. Each ethnic group wants to exercise its power and desire to control, and those in the minority often feel powerless.

LANGUAGE

The Ukrainian language is an East Slavic language, as are Russian and Belarusian. The alphabet differs slightly from Russian, but the two languages are mutually intelligible—that is, readers of one can read and speak the other, at least to a degree. The Ukrainian language is the official language of the country, but it is not the only language spoken by Ukrainians. Russian is widely spoken, especially in the eastern part of the country.

The Slavic languages are part of the Indo-European linguistic family believed to have originated in the Anatolia region (present-day Turkey) and from there spread in various directions. Linguistic subfamilies of Indo-European branched eastward to India and westward into Europe.

Language has played an important role in Ukrainian history, as it has in many countries throughout the world. Ukrainians used the language as a basis for ethnic self-identification. Throughout the nineteenth and twentieth centuries, minor groups searching for independence would rely on linguistic differences as a catalyst for the spread of nationalistic feelings. Similar to West and South Slavs who sought independence from the Habsburg Monarchy, Ukrainians sought to gain independence from the Russian Empire. Conquerors often forbade the teaching of Ukrainian in schools and its use in official, governmental business. By restricting the use of the language, rulers have tried to eliminate the sense of national self-belonging of the Ukrainian people. One of the first measures passed by the Ukrainian legislature on its course to independence from the USSR was to make Ukrainian the official language. In the parts of the country with large Russian populations, however, the Russian language is also widely spoken. Russian represents a *lingua franca* in the lands of the former Soviet Union. It is used as a language of trade and general communication among diverse peoples speaking different languages.

RELIGION

Like language, religion can be a unifying element in a country, and a conquering state may suppress it in order to solidify its power. Ukraine has a unique religion in the Uniate Church, also called the Ukrainian (or Greek) Catholic Church. It came into existence in the late sixteenth century and was influenced by foreign rule. Poland and Lithuania, whose people were Roman Catholics, dominated the people of western Ukraine at that time. By agreement, the Ukrainian Orthodox bishops accepted the leadership of the pope in Rome without giving up their familiar worship and ritual. The Uniate Church, therefore, practices Greek Orthodox forms of worship while acknowledging the pope in Rome as its leader. At that time, Russian influence in eastern Ukraine was growing, and there was no change to the Orthodox religion of the Cossacks.

In the late 1920s, during a time when Russian dominance of Ukraine was comparatively weak, the people formed an Orthodox Church with leadership in Kiev. It was called the Ukrainian Autocephalous Orthodox Church (UAOC). Following World War II, under Stalin and the USSR, the UAOC was outlawed along with the Uniate Church, which had been revived after being suppressed by the tsars. The Russian Orthodox Church, with its leaders in Moscow, took over the property of the Uniate Church.

Although the Uniate religion could not be practiced openly after 1948, people continued to practice in secret. In the late 1980s, as Soviet control loosened, the church around Lviv became an open rallying point for Ukrainian activists seeking independence. Because of its history, the Uniate Church has always been strongest in western Ukraine, centered in Lviv. It now has an estimated 4.5 million members. Uniate

Patriarch Filaret, whose secular name is Mykhailo Denysenko, leads a prayer at Saint Volodymyr Catherdal in Kiev. Patriarch Filaret is the head of the Ukrainian Orthodox Church of the Kyiv Patriarchate, which, along with the Russian Orthodox Church, is one of the two major Orthodox churches in Ukraine.

priests are the only Catholic priests in the world who can get married. In addition to the Uniate Church, the Ukrainian Orthodox Church (UOC, formerly the Russian Orthodox

Church) recognizes the Church leadership in Moscow, while the UAOC leaders are in Kiev.

The Roman Catholic Church is strongest in western Ukraine. This reflects the region's heritage of the strongly Roman Catholic Polish and Austro-Hungarian empires. It has an estimated 1.5 million members.

Religious holidays in Ukraine are celebrated on the Julian calendar, not the Gregorian calendar. The Julian calendar, named for Julius Caesar, who instituted it in the first century A.D., was based on an incorrect calculation of the length of a year. The cumulative effect of this over many years was that months got out of step with the climatic seasons. A new and better calendar, devised by Pope Gregory XIII, came into use in 1582. It adjusted the old calendar by 10 days, and should stay correct through many years. Even so, church festivals in the Orthodox faith follow the Julian calendar. So, for instance, Christmas is January 7, instead of December 25.

In Crimea, people of the Tatar community are Muslims. Their ancestors—the Golden Horde—adopted Islam in the fourteenth century. The people of Crimea recognized the supremacy of the Ottoman Empire in the late fifteenth century, and the Crimean Tatars also trace their ancestry to these Turkic peoples.

Historically, Ukraine has had an important Jewish community. At the beginning of World War II, approximately 3 million Jews lived in Ukraine, equivalent to about 20 percent of the world's Jewish people and 60 percent of Soviet Jewish population. They suffered greatly, however, in the tragic events of the Holocaust. In western Ukraine, only about 2 percent of the Jewish population survived. Today, Ukraine has about 500,000 Jewish people, approximately one percent of its population.

THE ARTS

Ukraine has a long and flourishing artistic tradition. Literature exists from as early as the tenth century. The *Tale of Bygone Years* from the eleventh century tells the story of the founding of Kiev by Kyi and his brothers and sister. Through the centuries of suppression, Ukrainian authors and poets have promoted independence for Ukraine. Taras Shevchenko (1814–1861) is a national hero, a painter, and a writer who suffered for his published work. He was born a serf, but his natural gifts were encouraged as a young man, and he was sent to study painting in St. Petersburg, Russia. His writings helped make the Ukrainian language well regarded for popular and influential literature. Because of his writings denouncing tsarist Russia, he was banished to Siberia for 10 years. However, the tradition of nationalistic writing continued and was an important factor driving the movement for independence.

Another art form with visible heritage in Ukraine is architecture. An early example is Saint Sophia Cathedral in Kiev, built between 1017 and 1031. Although its original Byzantine design is evident, it has been added to and rebuilt over the centuries, so that little of the original structure remains. Nevertheless, its many domes and side bell towers are a symbol of Kiev, and Saint Sophia Cathedral and the related monastic buildings have been recognized with the designation as a World Heritage Site by the United Nations Educational, Scientific, and Cultural Organization (UNESCO).

Architectural styles of the many ages are represented in churches throughout Ukraine. In Lviv are Renaissance-style buildings of the sixteenth century, reflecting the western European influences in that part of the country. The historic center of Lviv is Ukraine's other designated World Heritage Site.

A traditional form of the Ukrainian visual arts is the icon, a small picture painted on wood depicting a religious theme. Icons were painted during and following the eleventh century, soon after the Kievan Rus leaders adopted Christianity. Churches and museums display historic pieces.

Folk arts and crafts are plentiful. They exist in the hand embroidery work on blouses, belts, table linen, and skirts, and also in ceramic tableware. Parts of the Carpathian Mountain region are known for their carved wooden tools, furniture, and other items. Hand-painted eggs are a tradition that originated in Ukraine, although they are often associated with Russia. The Easter egg, called *pysanka*, traditionally was a dyed egg. Now the eggs may be made of stone, wood, or clay. They are elaborately decorated with paint or dye, often with a coating of wax used to separate color bands in dyeing. They may have simple lines and dots or elaborate geometric designs or floral patterns. The eggs of the different parts of the country may display patterns peculiar to the various regions.

Classical ballet developed in the region, and it later incorporated themes from local culture. Folk dances today often draw on Cossack tradition with movements like the "duck-kick." Classical music, opera, and ballet are performed extensively in Ukraine today.

In summary, Ukrainian culture includes traits that are also displayed in other cultures. It is, perhaps, the special combination of these traits that is distinctively Ukrainian. Conquerors through the centuries have recognized the national importance of the Ukrainian language and the Uniate Church by suppressing them and forbidding their use. Thus, even since independence, the Uniate faith is no longer dominant throughout the country, and in certain parts of Ukraine, the majority of local people do not speak the Ukrainian language.

The influence of neighboring countries is apparent in different parts of Ukraine—Poland in the west, Russia in the east, the Muslim community in the south. Since Ukraine was part of the Soviet Union for most of the twentieth century, it may be difficult to isolate the new country as being distinct from its former links. Much like the Easter egg, Borscht, the beet-based soup, is usually associated with Russia, but it probably originated in Ukraine.

Ukrainians describe themselves as openhearted and welcoming to visitors. Although they have fought for independence at various times in the twentieth century, they do not consider themselves militaristic, and as a people, they are peace loving. A set of cultural traits that is unique to all Ukraine, and to only Ukraine, is difficult to identify, but a special blend and pattern of traits exists throughout the country.

5

Government and Politics

A s the USSR's hold was weakening in the late twentieth century and change was in the air, the people of Ukraine demonstrated their solidarity one day in 1990—an estimated 500,000 held hands in a human chain that extended along a highway for more than 300 miles (483 kilometers)! With the chain, they marked the line where eastern and western Ukrainian republics had united in 1919, demonstrating the peoples' strong desire for a unified country of Ukraine and thus protesting Soviet domination. When the opportunity came to vote for their freedom, 84 percent cast their ballots in the general election in December 1991. Not surprisingly, more than 90 percent of the voters favored independence from the USSR. The new country of Ukraine came into being with the clear intent of and desire by its people to become a unified state among the world's nations.

Since independence, however, there have been multiple trials, tribulations, and triumphs during Ukraine's evolution as a nation-state—

and more can be expected. While the constitution and government structure are *centripetal* (unifying) forces, not surprisingly there is friction. In Crimea, the links with Russia are particularly strong and may act as a *centrifugal* force, pulling Crimea away from the center. The relative strength of the unifying versus divisive elements will have an important influence on the future of the Ukrainians. Ethnic groups' desire to govern themselves can be a very strong force of dissention in a culturally divided land.

Ukraine started the independence period with secure borders, a position that many nations have lacked historically. Ukraine assumed the borders that had defined it as a republic within the USSR. Its neighbors to the west, Poland, Hungary, and Romania, quickly determined they liked having Ukraine as a protective buffer nation between themselves and Russia. The people of Crimea with Russian heritage have voiced a desire to have Crimea return to Russia. In the late 1990s, however, under the terms of the Treaty of Friendship, Cooperation and Partnership, Russia affirmed the existing borders, in effect renouncing any claim to Crimea. Moldova, a former Soviet republic, is squeezed between Ukraine and Romania. Originally annexed by Russia in 1812, Moldova returned to its Romanian roots in 1918 before becoming a Soviet republic after World War II. Like Ukraine, the Republic of Moldova gained its independence in 1991.

STRUCTURE OF GOVERNMENT

Ukraine's administrative structure includes 24 *oblasts*, or political subdivisions, plus the Autonomous Crimean Republic. This "autonomous republic" designation is based on cultural differences. It recognizes the large Russian population of Crimea, the fact that the Russian language is more widely used than Ukrainian, and the importance of Russian culture and economic links with Russia in this portion of the country. It was also a political decision made to prevent any potential growth of separatist tendencies among Crimea's population.

Leonid Kuchma, pictured here testing traditional Ukrainian bread and salt while campaigning shortly before he was reelected in 1999, served as president of Ukraine from 1994 to 2005. Like most leaders of former Soviet republics, Kuchma was once a high-ranking member of the Communist Party.

Ukraine's first president, Leonid Kravchuk, was elected in 1991. The former Communist Party official ran for reelection in 1994, but was defeated by his former prime minister, Leonid Kuchma, who would go on to serve as president until 2005. As in other republics of the former Soviet Union, most new leaders were essentially members of the existing Communist structure. Following independence, Kravchuk adopted the program of Rukh (the People's Movement of Ukraine), an organization that had promoted independence and had become a political party. One of his most important decisions was to set a course for economic reform that included a market-driven, rather than a centrally controlled, economy.

A constitution was adopted in 1996. The unicameral legislature (consisting of one chamber, or body), or parliament, is called the Supreme Council, or Supreme Rada. Its 450 members are elected to a four-year term (in comparison, the U.S. House of Representatives has 435 members). The Presidium is a small group of 19 members of the Supreme Council that acts for the Supreme Council between sessions. It also rules on constitutional questions. (In the United States, the Supreme Court does this.)

The executive branch of the government consists of the president, who is the chief of state; the cabinet; and the prime minister, who is the head of government. Presidents are elected by direct vote of the people to five-year terms and are limited to two terms in office. A prime minister is nominated by the president, but must be confirmed by the parliament. The president also appoints the members of the cabinet who also must be confirmed by the Supreme Council. The prime minister heads the cabinet, and together they manage the administration of the government. Friction can exist between the president and prime minister, who can be dismissed from office by the president. The president can veto legislation, but a two-thirds vote by the Rada can override a veto. The Ukrainian Supreme Court is the highest court in the judicial system. Parliament elects its five judges for five-year terms. The Supreme Court administers the country's judicial system.

Until the late 1980s, the only legal political party was the Communist Party. It was banned in 1991, but again became legal in 1993 as one of many parties. Surprisingly, perhaps, in a country that had just gained its independence, the Communist Party was particularly strong. Its leaders, in fact, promoted close connections with Russia, and even advocated dual citizenship.

In 1999, approximately 70 different political parties, many with strong regional interests, had candidates who ran for parliamentary positions. Because of this, bills proposing reforms are often blocked. Relatively few Ukrainians, however, are registered party members. A change in the distribution of seats in parliament may lead to more influence by effective parties. Each party with more than 4 percent of the total vote receives proportional representation in one-half of the seats in parliament. The winning candidates in the various voting districts hold the other half of the seats.

The strong political influence of traditional circles of power has recently been broken in Ukraine. For more than a decade following independence, the country's political identity changed little. A structure inherited from the old Soviet system was still in place. Western-style democracy, still new to Ukrainians, and the process of public officials' accountability are traits that can develop slowly. Changes usually occur only when a new generation of people who do not live with the burden of the past becomes of voting age. In the minds of many young Ukrainians, 1991 is ancient history. Their eyes are fixed on the future rather than the past and they demand change.

In 2004, demands for change transformed Ukraine's political scene when the majority of voters supported former Prime Minister Viktor Yushchenko, in his presidential bid. Pro-Western and business oriented, Yushchenko won the presidency in a runoff against then Prime Minister Viktor Yanukovich, who received Moscow's endorsement. As one of the most popular politicians in the country, Yushchenko pledged to make political and economic reforms. The quality of life of ordinary Ukrainians had grown very slowly since independence and his message was well accepted. Elections, however, portrayed Ukraine as a country politically divided, because most of eastern Ukraine voted for Yanukovich, while western regions overwhelmingly supported Yushchenko. After a triumphant election victory, the Ukrainian president's energy is being directed toward bringing the country closer to the European

Union. Cleaning up the old political structure proved to be a difficult task. Not even a year after assuming power, the new president was accused of failing to take a stand against the old system. This led to a power struggle, accusations of corruption, and—as is often said in American politics—"politics as usual." Even his longtime ally and the country's most popular female politician and vital pre-election force, Yuliya Tymoshenko, broke her alliance with Yushchenko.

MILITARY

The president of Ukraine is the commander in chief of the armed forces. In 1991, at the time of independence, the country had a military force exceeding 700,000. By 1999, however, this number was reduced to about 350,000. Initially, most of the top officers were former Soviet officers; however, most of them were soon replaced and today nearly all of the top military positions are held by Ukrainians.

Today, Ukraine still has one of Europe's largest armies. It is, however, in need of more modern equipment. Although as a Soviet republic Ukraine had a large nuclear arsenal, in 1994 it agreed to give up its nuclear weapons. They were shipped to Russia to be destroyed. At the same time, the United States and Russia agreed to secure Ukraine's borders should they be threatened. Maintaining a large nuclear arsenal of about 1,300 missiles was not an option for Ukraine in the early 1990s; it was costly and geopolitically sensitive. Thus Ukraine, much like another former Soviet republic, Kazakhstan, decided to opt out of being in a selective club of nuclear powers. The country itself possesses the ability for production of material needed for nuclear arms, but the majority of uranium is being exported, mainly to Russia. In 2006, Ukraine announced that it might begin enriching uranium for civil purposes (nuclear power plants), which immediately raised eyebrows in both Moscow and Washington.

Although Ukraine has one of Europe's largest armies, the former Soviet satellite is no longer a nuclear power. In 1994, Ukraine signed a Nuclear Nonproliferation Treaty with Russia and transferred its remaining nuclear weapons to Russia. Here, Ukrainian military cadets march during a parade in Kiev in October 2004, commemorating the 60th anniversary of liberation from Nazi Germany.

INTERNATIONAL AGREEMENTS

Ukraine is a member of a number of international organizations. It was one of 51 charter members to sign the United Nations Charter in 1945. When the UN was being organized, Ukraine and what is now Belarus were given seats in this global political organization. Although Ukraine was not independent, it played a significant role in drafting the charter's preamble and first article. In 1999, Ukraine was elected to a two-year term on the UN Security Council.

Shortly after independence in 1991, Ukraine joined with Russia and Belarus to form the Commonwealth of independent States (CIS). Since then, eight other former Soviet republics have joined. This group provides a forum for discussion, but it does not have formal authority to act in political and economic matters.

Although Ukraine is not a member of the North Atlantic Treaty Organization (NATO), it cooperates with that organization. It joined NATO's Partnership for Peace program in 1994, and its armed forces have participated in NATO peacekeeping missions in the Balkans.

Ukraine helped form GUUAM (Georgia, Ukraine, Uzbekistan, Azerbaijan, Moldova), an organization of former Soviet republics that are inclined to look toward the Western world for leadership as they work toward building a better future for their countries.

Equally important to the people of Ukraine is their relationship with Russia. The economies were totally integrated prior to 1991 with interconnecting roads, railroads, and pipelines. In the late 1990s, the two countries signed the Treaty of Friendship, Cooperation and Partnership. However, despite this pact, several issues have created conflict between the two nations. More recently, in late fall 2005, Russia announced that it was going to stop distributing natural gas to Ukraine. To resume shipments, Gazprom (the Russian state-controlled company) demanded a major increase in the price of natural gas. Gas prices, Russia argued, represented heavily subsidized Soviet-era prices, rather than modern era market prices.

Ukraine aspires to join the European Union (EU) and has a Partnership and Cooperation Agreement (PCA) in place with that organization. Under the PCA guidelines, however, a good deal of work must be done before Ukraine qualifies for full membership.

The United States quickly recognized Ukraine as an independent country and established an embassy in Kiev in January 1992. It is committed to helping Ukraine during its sometimes difficult transition from a newly independent former Soviet republic to a lively democracy and has provided financial aid.

Much of this assistance has been to help build a market economy and to aid people in great need in an economy that is still making the transition from centralized control.

The United States also provides assistance in the form of exchange programs, in which U.S. specialists, such as business people, individuals who provide technical assistance, and those who help develop civil society, help make the transition to democracy a bit easier for Ukrainians. In addition, various academic exchange programs exist, including those that involve college faculty and students from both countries.

A number of U.S. government agencies also are trying to help Ukraine build solid institutions. Help is being offered to develop a criminal-justice system, drug-enforcement programs, reliable tax systems, health-care delivery, and military training. The United States also is helping to provide attractive employment in peaceful research for former nuclear weapons scientists.

Since independence, Ukraine has been united in its quest to establish a democratic state. The world community welcomed the new country with good wishes and tangible aid. Institutions of democracy were rather promptly established and, for the most part, they have functioned as intended. The obstacles, however, are formidable; possibly the greatest challenge is in establishing a strong economy.

6

Ukraine's Economy

U kraine has most of the resources it needs to develop a strong and diversified economy. It has excellent soils and rich coal and iron resources. It also has an educated population capable of producing a wealth of varied goods and services. For now, however, as in many other former Communist countries, the potentials are slow to develop. After a long period when its economy and government were controlled by the state, Ukraine requires some time to successfully transform into an affluent nation.

Economies can be measured in many ways. One is the importance of work that different people do. Another is the way wealth and production are controlled and distributed. A country's economic strength is often measured by its total production. This measure, called Gross Domestic Product (GDP), is the value of all goods and services produced by a country in a year. (It does not count the "shadow economy," or items that are not taxed and do not get counted in most government statistics.) As Ukraine develops its market economy, its traditional agricultural segment is of less importance than manufacturing, sales, services, and other businesses.

Under the Soviet government, all planning was centralized. Each manufacturing facility and mining operation was given quotas for production and all goods, regardless of quality, were assured a buyer. This is often termed a *command economy*, or a *planned economy*. Transforming this structure and way of thinking to the "supply and demand" nature of a market-driven economy has been difficult in Ukraine. Immediately after independence and continuing through most of the 1990s, economic growth declined. Since then, however, the country has managed to recover from the economic downturn.

SECTORS OF THE ECONOMY
Agriculture

Throughout much of its history, Ukraine has relied on its fertile black Chernozem soils as the backbone of its agriculture-based economy. During the Soviet era, Ukraine produced more than one-fourth of the agricultural output of the USSR, including as much as 50 percent of its sugar beet production. It was one of the world's leading *breadbaskets*. This term, however, may have become outdated during the 1990s. During this period, agricultural activity declined, and it is no longer the most important segment of Ukraine's economy. As the importance of industry, commerce, and services expands, agriculture may never again be the major contributor to the country's economy. But tremendous potential exists for agricultural production to expand and help support an ever-growing world population. Approximately one-third of Ukraine's land is under cultivation. The country is the world's largest producer of sugar beets and a major producer of wheat, corn, other grains and cereals, and potatoes. Farmers grow winter wheat, barley, winter rye, buckwheat, and millet. Sunflowers are a crop

Agricultural exports are an important part of Ukraine's economy. The country is one of the world's largest producers of wheat and ranks in the top 10 in wheat exports. Here, a Ukrainian farmer harvests his wheat crop on a farm south of Kiev.

common in the steppes, raised because the seeds produce valuable cooking oil. The agricultural business also includes food processing and production of cereals, sugar, milk, and other products.

Agricultural products are important exports of Ukraine; Russia and other CIS countries are the primary buyers. Export crops include grains, sugar, legumes, dairy products, meat products, vegetables, and oil. Ukraine's leading trade partners for its agricultural products will most likely continue to be Russia and other former Soviet republics. The European Union, dominated by the countries of Western Europe, is protective of its members' agricultural production and markets, and most likely will maintain import taxes and other barriers to Ukrainian agricultural products.

In the drier southern part of the country, crops of tomatoes, peppers, other vegetables, and melons are grown with the help of irrigation. Grapes also are grown for making wines. Throughout the country, cattle, sheep, poultry, and pigs are raised. Bees are kept for honey and also because they pollinate various crops. Crimea, with its Mediterranean climate, is especially well suited for orchards and vineyards.

Fishing

Traditionally, fishing has been an important source of food in Ukraine. The Black Sea and the Sea of Azov have yielded large catches, as have several of the major rivers. The fishing industry has declined in recent years, however, because of severe pollution in the country's rivers, lakes, and seas. For example, the Dnieper River has more than 60 species of fish, including catfish, perch, pike, chub, carp, sturgeon, and herring, but it is so polluted with human and industrial waste and agricultural runoff that eating its fish is discouraged.

Mining and Industry

Ukraine has a number of mineral deposits, which are basic economic building blocks. Rich coal deposits were discovered in 1721 in eastern Ukraine, in the area of the Donetsky Basin (Donbas). The Donbas region, north and east of the city of Donetsk (Donetske), has been one of the world's most important mining and manufacturing centers since the 1880s.

Huge iron ore deposits are found in the central part of Ukraine, west of the big bend of the Dnieper River. The city of Krivoy Rog (Kryvy Rih), located at the junction of the Inhulets and Saksahan rivers, became an important iron-works center in the early 1880s. A railroad linked these iron ore deposits with the coal of Donbas, approximately 250 miles away. Together,

Donbas and Krivoy Rog became a booming industrial and manufacturing region. By about 1913, Donbas produced more than 85 percent of all Russian coal and more than 70 percent of Russian pig iron.

But ironworks eventually gave way to steel mills. A required ingredient in steel is manganese, and deposits of this mineral are located not far from Krivoy Rog, at Nikopol. It is one of the world's largest deposits of manganese and is most conveniently located near other necessary ingredients for the mills.

And while Donbas's coal deposits initially were readily available near the ground's surface, they have been mined for decades. Most coal reserves now are deep underground, averaging 1,150 to 1,300 feet (350–400 meters) below the surface, and coal production has declined in recent years.

In addition to these natural resources, deposits of other mineral ores exist in Ukraine, including titanium, bauxite, and gold. Clay is used in ceramics, pottery, and bricks. A rather unusual mineral deposit found in Ukraine is salt. Crimea has large salt deposits, some up to 600 feet (180 meters) thick in places.

The country's manufacturing plants were severely damaged during World War II. But when they were rebuilt, they were modernized to meet the technological standards of the time. During the second half of the twentieth century, Donbas became one of the world's major industrial production areas for metallurgy and heavy industrial equipment. A chemical industry also was developed, including the manufacture of plastics.

Nearly all of Ukraine's heavy industrial facilities were established during the Soviet period. They were designed to be an integral part of the USSR's nationwide industrial complex. Transportation facilities linked Ukrainian plants and mines with other parts of the USSR. But there were few routes joining Ukraine with its European neighbors to the west. As with its railroads and electric lines, the country's pipelines also carried oil and natural gas to the USSR. This northeast orientation poses a problem: Ukraine's infrastructure (means of delivery) continues to isolate the country and its economy somewhat from western Europe.

Energy

In the mid-twentieth century, Ukraine was a major producer of natural gas, but in recent years production has declined. It must now import petroleum products, primarily from Russia. Almost half of its electrical energy comes from fossil fuels, while the rest is provided by nuclear plants and hydroelectric generation. In terms of electrical energy, contemporary issues are not related to production. Rather, the primary problem rests with an aging and inefficient distribution network that has seen little improvement since the Soviet era.

Other Businesses

Some new industries are now being developed in Ukraine. For instance, near Kiev, factories produce cameras, precision tools, clothing, watches, chemicals, and aircraft. Former military production facilities are being converted to make tractors and consumer goods. Donbas manufacturing has developed and changed over time and consumer goods are now made in the area, including refrigerators.

The high-tech industry is a rapidly growing economic sector in Ukraine, one that has developed essentially since independence. Well-known computer product manufacturers active in the market include the American firms IBM, Dell, Apple, Hewlett-Packard, Intel, and Microsoft. Many of these companies have assembly plants in Ukraine.

Most computer buyers are government offices and businesses; home use of computers is still quite limited. Software development and manufacture is also a problem. Ukraine does not have strict laws protecting intellectual property rights, which means that people make copies of software without paying full price to the manufacturer and without fear of being prosecuted for theft. An enforceable law protecting intellectual property rights would stimulate the legal software industry.

THE ECONOMY SINCE INDEPENDENCE

The economic transition since 1991 has been difficult for the people of Ukraine. Before independence, as part of the centrally controlled economy of the Soviet Union, the government established production targets. In this command economy, markets (buyers) were assured. Products were delivered as instructed, and the recipient had to accept them whether or not they were needed. Factories did not compete with one another. Therefore, there was no incentive to develop and install more efficient production methods or, indeed, to maintain existing equipment. When the USSR disintegrated, there were no longer assured buyers for Ukrainian products. Obsolete and inefficient plants were not competitive in the world market.

Politicians spoke of tying Ukrainian industry to Western markets, but that could not be accomplished overnight. The people who managed plants had traditional ties with Russia. And many of them had personal financial incentives for maintaining their state-owned facilities. While national leaders saw the need to convert state-owned factories to corporations owned through stock held by individual citizens, they found their policies thwarted by entrenched bureaucrats and plant managers. Modernizing Soviet-era factories requires a sizable investment in new machinery, and Ukraine still lacks sufficient investment capital. It also needs considerable time to train new managers. Again, even in this context, cultural change requires time and a new generation of educated people who never experienced the burden of a non-free market society.

In attempting to reform agricultural production, the government tried to break up the huge collective farms. It wanted individuals to own farms, raise crops, and sell their harvests—and, most important, to keep the money from the sale of their products. The political leaders reasoned that if people were to benefit directly from their own labor, then they would use the most efficient methods and maximize the profits of their work. There were obstacles, however. The former Communists who were in charge of the collectives initially resisted such reforms, because they had a financial stake in the continuation of the old ways. And the farm workers had followed central instructions for so long that they had no experience in making their own decisions and being in charge of their own farms. Although privatization of agriculture is taking place, the conversion has been slower than initially anticipated.

About 10 years after independence, Ukraine abolished the remaining collective farms and forgave past debts that farmers owed the government. The people who worked on each collective received a designated portion of land for their own. They could sell the land, or they could add to it by buying land from neighbors. The workers on some collectives decided to continue to work the land in common. They formed cooperative associations in which they all share the work and the profits. This resulted in the agricultural economy growing more than 20 percent in 2001 alone and the positive trend has continued. The tendency now is increasingly toward smaller farms, and it is the privately owned units that are now producing most of Ukraine's vegetables, fruit, meat, eggs, and dairy products.

Converting the coal-mining industry to a market system also has been difficult. Mine workers have often gone on strike, and many of the mines are unprofitable, inefficient, and dangerous. An average 300 miners die each year in tragic mining accidents, but the mines employ many people and the government subsidizes the operation. That is, the coal cannot be sold for enough money to pay the workers' wages and other expenses, so the government provides the additional funds needed. To close the mines would put a lot of people out of work, and this is politically unacceptable. So the mines continue to operate in a controlled environment. Beginning in about 2000, a few of the unprofitable mines were closed.

Some international aid has helped the miners who lost their jobs. Many of them are being trained to find different kinds of employment.

Privatization

One key aspect of encouraging investment in Ukraine is its progress in privatizing firms that were owned by the state during the Soviet period. The Ukrainian government issued "privatization certificates" in the mid-1990s, and by year-end 1996 had distributed them to approximately 85 percent of Ukrainians. The certificates can be exchanged for shares in businesses as the government converts firms to private ownership, thereby privatizing the state-owned enterprises.

By mid-1999, about 45,000 small businesses, such as restaurants and small shops, had converted to private companies. Larger firms were harder to convert, but 7,850 of these (more than 70 percent) were in private ownership. When the government no longer controls an industry, competitive opportunities can open up with other manufacturers or suppliers stepping in to bid for the business.

Ukrtelecom, the Ukrainian Telecommunications Company, is an example. It owns all transmission facilities and administers the wire line infrastructure. It is a huge firm, and there is much debate over whether it should be converted from government to private ownership. Privatization would encourage investment, which is needed to modernize and upgrade facilities. But politicians who fear giving up control of such a large and important industry have resisted this step. Potential growth in the telecommunications business is a foregone conclusion with the rapidly growing demand for fax, e-mail, mobile phones, and Internet services.

After independence, some people were in a position to benefit in inappropriate ways. People in charge of factories, for instance, received government money for the factories, but managed to convert it into personal wealth rather than reinvest-

After the fall of the Soviet Union in 1991, private businesses began to fill the void left by those formerly controlled by the state. Street-side vendors, such as those pictured here in downtown Kiev, can now freely sell their goods without fear of government reprisal.

ing it. Sometimes people, often termed *oligarchs*, transferred the money out of Ukraine. This was not helpful at a time when the country needed investment capital and was trying to attract foreign firms to establish businesses. Sometimes the oligarchs turned their businesses into illegal "underground" enterprises, for which they did not apply for required government licenses and pay taxes. Corruption was widespread in the early 1990s, and it continues to create many problems today. In fact, the country ranks near the bottom of several indices of corruption in the world's countries. This makes it difficult for Ukraine to regain a reputation for honorable dealing—a trait that legitimate investors insist upon in business activities.

Currency

Shortly after independence, as economic activity declined, the government failed to control the stability of its currency. In

1993, there was a time of hyperinflation, in which money rapidly lost its value. One month a unit of currency would buy a loaf of bread; the next month that unit of currency was enough to purchase only half a loaf. High inflation also wiped out the value of people's savings. This was particularly hard on people near the end of their working careers who had saved some money to support their retirement.

In 1996, a new currency was introduced called the *hryvnia* (UAH). It was stable for about two years at U.S.$1 = 2 UAH (a person could buy one U.S. dollar for two hryvnias). But in 1998, the Russian economy suffered a severe decline. Because of the close economic connection between the two countries, Ukraine also experienced a sharp decline in economic activity. In response, the government devalued the currency by about half. At the end of 1999, its value was only U.S.$1 = 5.33 UAH, but the government soon after managed to stabilize the currency. At the beginning of 2006, this ratio was still about 1:5.

Individual Purchasing Power

One measure of the economic success of a country is the level of its citizens' personal income. Wages of most Ukrainians are low, and the government is notoriously far behind in paying workers in government facilities. As a result, in 1998, 40 percent of Ukrainians were living below the poverty line (although the figure has now dropped to below 30 percent).

Gross national income (GNI) is the total value of all goods and services produced within a country, including the net income earned by citizens who live abroad. Purchasing power parity (PPP) converts this number to "international" dollars. That is, it takes into account the cost of living in different places and makes it possible to compare income consistently. An "international dollar" in Ukraine has the same relationship to the cost of items in Ukraine as a U.S. dollar has in the United States. Gradual economic revitalization has helped elevate this category in recent years. For example, while PPP in Ukraine in

1999 was barely above $3,000, by 2005, it had doubled to more than $6,800.

International Links

The United States and other countries, as well as international organizations like the World Bank, are trying to do business with the Ukrainians. Trading ties are being built with countries of western Europe. Agencies of the U.S. government are prepared to help businesses that want to establish operations in Ukraine. These include Coca-Cola, Pepsi, McDonald's, and some other firms with familiar consumer products. Other firms include large companies in agribusiness, such as Cargill, and in heavy industry, such as John Deere and Boeing.

The World Bank has agreed to lend money to Ukraine on very favorable terms at a low interest rate and with many years before repayment is due. As a condition of the loans, the World Bank requires Ukraine to meet certain benchmarks in developing a market economy. For instance, it must transform some manufacturing plants from state ownership into private corporations. When Ukraine does not meet the benchmarks, the World Bank does not increase the loans. In the 10 years following 1991, the World Bank loaned Ukraine $2.2 billion of a total of $2.9 billion that it had agreed to lend when the conditions were met.

Another cause of slow economic growth is the ever-expanding market for pirated and counterfeited U.S. goods. U.S. law requires all trading partners to respect U.S. patents, trademarks, and "intellectual property rights." This law is designed to stop the pirating (stealing or illegally reproducing) of U.S. products, such as CDs by popular singers. It means that CDs may not be copied and sold without paying "royalties" to the U.S. companies that produce them. If Ukraine will not pass a strong law protecting intellectual property rights and enforce it, then the United States will not allow some Ukrainian products to enter its market.

Trade continues with Russia, a country with which Ukraine's economy has been tied for many decades. This relationship, regardless of periodical hiccups, is promoted as Ukraine seeks ways to improve the situations of its citizens.

Many American corporations, such as McDonald's, Coca-Cola, and Pepsi, are entering the Ukrainian market. The old blends with the new in this photo where a McDonald's sign is pictured behind an Orthodox church in Kiev.

Shadow Economy

The term *shadow economy* includes economic activities such as illegal drug dealing and racketeering, and small family enterprises that avoid paying taxes. The shadow economy that is most troubling, however, is the commonplace cheating by sizeable firms that do not pay taxes. In Ukraine, the shadow economy is estimated to account for as much as one-half of the country's total economic activity! This represents a huge amount of money being exchanged outside of the formal, legal frame-work. The loss is very damaging to the country's economy. It also takes a severe toll on citizens' confidence in their government and on the national psyche itself.

People operate outside of the law for a variety of reasons. In Ukraine, taxes are quite high—as much as 90 percent of profits. Government bureaucrats who administer the laws may have a lot of discretion in how they make decisions, and this may cause bribery to be a way to get something done. Registering a business properly, for example, can be very time-consuming. Many corporate managers simply pay a bribe to speed up the process, rather than lose time better spent working to earn profits.

When people are disillusioned with the way their government works and when they avoid meeting requirements, then the whole rule of law can break down, with terrible consequences to a society. If the country is to succeed economically, the government absolutely must take strong action to reduce and ultimately eliminate the shadow economy. If taxes were lower, people might not mind paying them as much, especially if the government services supported by the taxes became more efficient. If officials were better paid, and if the rules were clear and evenly applied, then bribery might disappear. Ultimately, this would benefit the entire country, with all businesses being registered and paying taxes. It would also allow the country to collect more accurate data so that it can make more appropriate decisions about its economy.

Corruption

A problem related to the shadow economy is that of bureaucratic corruption. This is most troublesome to foreign companies considering investment in Ukraine, because the country has a reputation for being corrupt; government officials must be bribed before they will respond to a request for service. Organized crime also flourishes in Ukraine. This presence of massive corruption and formal criminal organizations discourages many businesses from becoming involved in Ukraine.

Ukraine has an abundance of natural resources, a well-educated populace, and a favorable location. It should be able to develop a thriving economy. Corruption that today stands in the way of achieving this goal simply cannot be allowed to exist.

7

Living in Ukraine Today

Today, many Ukrainians are focused on making a living, which can be difficult given the weak economy. Because of this weak economy, such industries as health care have been adversely affected; there is a shortage of public funds to maintain health clinics. A number of environmental concerns also occupy the attention of Ukrainians. The country has a great deal of pollution, including radioactive fallout caused by the nuclear disaster at Chernobyl in 1986.

About two-thirds of all Ukrainians live in cities. Regional differences are obvious, both in the urban centers around the country and in the rural communities. Travelers will find many places of interest in Ukraine. And, like many people around the world, Ukrainians are enthusiastic soccer fans!

EDUCATION

School begins for Ukrainian children when they are six or seven years old and is required for nine grades. Students can then go to a trade school for vocational or technical training or continue on in high school for another two years. High school graduates are then eligible to attend one of the country's state universities. Beginning in the fifth grade, students take annual exams in each subject. English is a mandatory subject for four to six years beginning in the fifth grade. There are also private schools and public day care and kindergarten are available. Ukraine is currently implementing a 12-year course of study in elementary and secondary schooling, which will be similar to the general educational system in many other countries.

The first institution of higher learning in Ukraine was the Kiev-Mohyla Academy in Kiev, founded in 1615. (The oldest institution of higher learning in the United States is Harvard University, founded in 1636.) Early students learned philosophy and theology, important topics of the times, and the school attracted scholars from many countries. It was much reduced in size and importance, however, by Tsar Peter I in the early 1700s, because of its nationalistic teachings. It rebounded later in that century, but became primarily a school for candidates for the clergy in the early 1800s. Since Ukraine's independence, it has been reinstated as a university of general education and is symbolic of the new importance of Ukrainian national spirit.

Ukraine's 99.7 percent adult literacy rate ranks among the highest in the world. Having almost an entire adult population that is able to read and write is a valuable human resource. Ukraine needs, however, to find a way to retain its people, who often, when able, move abroad in search of better opportunities. During the 1990s, an estimated 500,000 people left Ukraine. Most of these emigrants were among its best-educated citizens.

FOOD

A traveler in Ukraine would encounter a wide variety of local foods. A traditional Ukrainian dish, although often associated with Russia, is borscht. This red soup usually includes meat, beans, beets, cabbage, tomatoes, potatoes, carrots, and onions that are simmered together for hours. Borscht is often served topped with sour cream. Another traditional dish, *varenyky*, is a type of dumpling whose dough is rolled around a stuffing of meat or vegetables and which is then boiled or steamed for a long time. For the most part, Ukrainian cuisine is hearty, much like what is found throughout the European interior.

SPORTS

Football ("soccer") is a national pastime and passion. It is played in schools (both intra- and intermural), in club leagues, in a popular national league, and internationally. Dynamo-Kyiv is a well-known and highly ranked European team.

Ukrainian athletes enter international competition in a variety of events, and the country can boast of Olympic champions in gymnastics, figure skating, Greco-Roman wrestling, weight lifting, and boxing, among other sports. A gymnast from Kherson, Ukraine, named Larisa Latynina, competing on the Soviet team, won more Olympic medals than any other athlete. Between 1956 and 1964, she won medals in 18 events, including 9 gold medals in 1956. In the 1994 Winter Olympics in Lillehammer, Norway, the figure skater Oksana Baiul won the first gold medal for an independent Ukraine.

HEALTH

Ukraine's environmental and health problems reflect the challenges that face the new nation. Some of the human health problems are caused by environmental pollution. Respiratory ailments are caused by industrial pollution that sends particles into the air. This is especially bad in the heavily industrialized eastern part of the country near some of the big cities. Also, when water treatment facilities are inadequate, leaving water impure, it can carry bacteria that can cause diseases such as cholera. In 1994, there was a serious outbreak of cholera in Crimea.

Ukrainian figure skater Oksana Baiul wipes away a tear after she wins the gold medal for ladies figure skating at the 1994 Winter Olympic Games in Lillehammer, Norway. Baiul was the first Ukrainian to capture a gold medal for her country.

The number of people infected with HIV/AIDS in Ukraine is not large in comparison with some countries in the world, but the number of cases is growing rapidly. In 1994, 400 cases were reported. By 2004, the number of cases had risen to about 70,000. Lack of successful health-care management in early years contributed to this dramatic increase. In recent years, governmental measures began to provide better care, information, and education. The Ukrainian government and citizens are seriously concerned about cooperation with international organizations (for example, the United Nations, World Bank, and so forth) in fighting not only HIV/AIDS, but other diseases as well.

CHERNOBYL AND POLLUTION PROBLEMS

The place name associated with the world's greatest nuclear disaster, Chernobyl, is in Ukraine, approximately 80 miles (130 kilometers) north of Kiev. The failure of the nuclear reactor in 1986 is seared into the national consciousness of Ukrainians. On April 26, one of the reactors at the plant became unstable and exploded. The cause of the disaster was later attributed to human error, poor training and execution, and faulty design. Approximately 11 tons of radioactive particles were blown into the air. This is many times the radiation emitted when the United States dropped an atomic bomb on the Japanese city of Hiroshima in 1945.

Immediately after the explosion, no public announcement was made. At the time, the wind was blowing toward Belarus and the northwest. Several days later, Swedish scientists detected a sharp rise in atmospheric radiation and sounded an alert, and the Soviet government finally acknowledged the danger. By that time, a great many people experienced far greater exposure to radiation than they would have had they been evacuated promptly from the region. About 135,000 people were then evacuated from an area within an 18-mile (30-kilometer) radius of the plant.

The cleanup crews encased the damaged reactor in concrete, but after some years, there was evidence that the "sarcophagus" was deteriorating. Should it become unstable and

collapse, it could release a vast dust cloud of radioactive particles. It is estimated that approximately 600,000 people worked
in the cleanup effort. The debris and all the vehicles and equipment used in the cleanup have been buried in hundreds of sites
in the vicinity.

Thirty-one people died directly as a result of the Chernobyl
explosion. The long-term aftermath of this tragic event, however, has affected millions of people. Useful medical records
were not kept on people who worked in the cleanup effort, but
many workers were exposed to a far higher dose of radiation
than is normally considered safe. After the disaster, they moved
throughout the USSR and now cannot be traced in order to follow their medical histories.

It is estimated that approximately 5,000 people who worked
in the cleanup have died of radiation sickness. And an estimated
4.9 million people living in Ukraine, Belarus, and southwestern
Russia have been affected in some way by the nuclear pollution
(fallout) resulting from the explosion. More than 300 cases of
thyroid cancer among children, for example, were reported in
the nearby regions the first several years after the accident. This
is a very high number for this relatively rare disease.

The 18-mile-radius (30-kilometer-radius) area around
Chernobyl that was evacuated after the event remains closed to
the public. Today, approximately 15 percent of Ukraine's
national budget goes to costs associated with the Chernobyl disaster. This includes pensions supporting the early retirement of
the people who worked in the cleanup effort and whose health
deteriorated so much that they have been unable to work again.

The people who were evacuated were affected in other
ways, including experiencing significant psychological stress.
The disaster occurred in a farming area. Many of the rural people who were evacuated to apartment buildings in cities have
found it very difficult to adjust to life in an urban environment.
Some of them have returned to their homes near Chernobyl,
despite knowing that it is unsafe.

Due to the nuclear disaster at Chernobyl in 1986, Ukrainian school-children participate in safety drills on a regular basis. As a result of the disaster, many residents of Pripyat, just one mile from the nuclear plant, were moved to the town of Slavutich to avoid the nuclear fallout.

Scientists are studying how radiation exposure has affected plants and animals. Both Ukraine and Belarus are considering making the affected area a wildlife sanctuary. Consideration also has been given to storing spent nuclear fuel at Chernobyl. All the reactors at Chernobyl are now shut down. The United States has provided substantial amounts of aid to help assure that other nuclear power plants in Ukraine are safe.

The long-term contamination is one of the saddest results of the accident. People believe the land will be polluted for at least a century. Radioactive contaminants (cesium 137 radioisotope) have seeped into the topsoil. From there, they are picked up by water that feeds into the groundwater, which is the source of moisture for plants and animals. That chain then leads to the people who eat them. Radioactive silt is washed into the rivers and carried downstream. Sediment with radioactive particles is accumulating behind the dam on the Dnieper River located downstream of Chernobyl and just north of Kiev. The full extent of this pollution is not known. Kiev's Chernobyl Museum interprets this tragic event with photographs of cleanup crews at work and the repercussions of the nuclear disaster.

The Chernobyl accident helped bring about an environmental movement in Ukraine. (A strong reaction against the Soviet government because of the accident also strengthened the independence movement.) The ecological movement attracted scientists, journalists, and environmental activists from all across Ukraine. Since independence, a political party with an environmental platform, the Green Party, has developed. Although small, it does have representatives in parliament and keeps government officials alert to environmental issues.

BEYOND CHERNOBYL

Ukraine has severe environmental problems in addition to the contamination from Chernobyl. With all of its economic suffering for the first 10 years after independence, Ukraine has had little money to devote to environmental issues other than Chernobyl. One unfortunate legacy of Soviet industrial and military policy is pollution. Discharge from smokestacks in industrial areas cause respiratory problems. Cars typically burn leaded gas, and in cities this pollution is particularly pronounced. The runoff of pesticides and fertilizer from agricultural fields is detrimental to water quality. In rivers and lakes, it causes unnatural algae growth, which reduces dissolved oxygen in water so that fish, and the organisms they feed on, cannot survive. Sewage treatment plants often are inadequate, and the discharge of human waste from cities flows to the major rivers.

Historically, the Black Sea was a source of a vibrant fishing industry yielding dolphin, mackerel, anchovy, and sturgeon (producing caviar). The catch has declined dramatically, with a

sharp loss in jobs and revenues. Pollution has also been detrimental to the tourist business on Black Sea coastal towns and
beaches. To reverse the trend of growing pollution in the Black
Sea, many countries, including Ukraine, will have to work
together.

Many Ukrainians worry about environmental problems,
but there still exists the need to develop a widespread environmental consciousness. People raised under the Soviet mind-set
may not be aware of the environmentally damaging consequences of industrial activity. Laws that penalize polluters need
to be enforced. In some places, environmental subjects are
appearing in school curricula and university training. Some
environmental nongovernment organizations (NGOs) are
forming. The Worldwide Fund for Nature (WWF) participates
in a consortium of NGOs and other organizations focused on
the Danube River and in Ukraine on the Danube delta.

TRAVELING THE REGIONS

Many developing countries have a major city that dominates
urban life, a situation that can cause problems in providing
adequate housing, transportation, and utilities for residents.
Ukraine does not have an urban problem of this nature. Kiev,
although a large city, does not dominate the country's urban
centers. Five cities have populations greater than one million,
and these cities are located in different parts of the country.
They are Kiev, Kharkiv in the northeast, Dnepropetrovsk centrally located at the big bend of the Dniester River, Donetsk in
the industrial east, and Odessa in the south.

A traveler in Ukraine would notice regional differences that
reflect the country's different historic experiences and natural
landscapes. With two-thirds of Ukrainians living in cities, the
major urban centers are a microcosm of the country's various
regions. A traveler could see the range of cities and landscapes
by beginning in Kiev and making a loop to the southwest to
Lviv, then to the south to Odessa and Crimea, then to the

eastern manufacturing centers, and finally to the northern forests and lowlands.

Kiev

The capital and largest city is a major focal point of Ukrainian life today. Kiev is the center of government and has important industrial and scientific research institutions. It also houses major cultural and sporting events. The land around Kiev is relatively flat and forested under natural conditions. The city itself has much natural parkland, and new factories must locate outside the city beyond a greenbelt district.

Kiev has many sites and monuments associated with Ukrainian history. As previously mentioned, the domes of Saint Sophia Cathedral are a defining symbol of the city. The Podil section of Kiev, located along the riverbank below the bluff where the main part of town lies, has historically been the center of commerce.

The Caves Monastery, about two miles (three kilometers) south of the heart of Kiev, also dates to the Kievan Rus period. The complex includes several churches, other buildings, and underground caves where the monks lived. Mummified bodies of monks line the passageways in the caves. In addition to touring the caves, visitors can also see beautiful gold jewelry crafted by Greeks of Scythian times and found in burial mounds nearby.

Outside Kiev is a site associated with World War II atrocities and the Holocaust. In 1941, the Nazis ordered Jewish people of the city to assemble for transfer away from their homes. However, they were taken only a short distance to Babyn Yar and killed. About 34,000 people died in that massacre. Over the course of the next two years, thousands more died in the concentration camp there.

Lviv

Lviv is the major center in western Ukraine. A Galatian prince founded it as a fort on a hilltop in the mid-thirteenth century.

The site was selected as a fortification among the mountain passes of the Carpathians. From the ancient castle site, there is a 360-degree view of the city and environs. The architecture and other features of Lviv and western Ukraine reflect its Polish heritage.

The region near Lviv has forests, rivers, and lakes. The Dniester River originates in this area and flows to the Black Sea. Carpathian National Park is in the mountains not far from Lviv, and Ukrainians often hike and ski there. Forestry is an important industry, helping Lviv to become an important furniture-manufacturing center.

South of Lviv is the city of Ivano-Frankivsk, located in the northeastern foothills of the Carpathian Mountains. The region has natural resources of oil and gas, gold, and manganese. About 40 miles (65 kilometers) south of Lviv is Kolomyya, founded in the thirteenth century on the salt trade route between Galicia and the Black Sea. The town of Kolomyya is known as the cultural center of the Hutzuls culture, ethnic Ukrainians from the Carpathian Mountains. They are known for their traditional crafts of carved wooden tools, boxes, and furniture, as well as embroidered folk dresses. This is also the area of the Carpathian Biosphere Reserve, which protects Europe's last virgin beech forest.

In the far western reaches of Ukraine is the city of Uzhhorod, which has existed since at least A.D. 903. It is near the Ukrainian borders with Slovakia and Hungary and not far from Romania; many people in the city trace their heritage to these countries. This region, known as Transcarpathia, has deposits of iron and copper. Farmers raise cattle and sheep and the agricultural products of grapes, vegetables, and winter grains. Tourism is important to the area's economy, including winter ski resorts located in the mountains. Ukrainians calculate the center of Europe as being a point in these mountains near the town of Rakhov.

Odessa

The city of Odessa is a major port and is also known for its appealing beaches. Catherine the Great of Russia had the city rebuilt in the late eighteenth century after her forces conquered the area. It sits on a high promontory. One of its distinctive features is a broad stairway, called the Potemkin Steps, which lead from the city center to the seashore. With 12 flights of 20 steps each, it is an impressive approach to the Black Sea.

The opera house in Odessa is considered one of the most beautiful in Europe. In addition to being a cultural center, the city has several important academic institutions and film studios.

Odessa's economy has fared better than many other Ukrainian cities since independence. Privatization has proceeded more rapidly and people enjoy a higher standard of living than many of their countrymen. Machine building is an important industry, as is oil refining. The city is also a resort center. People come to "take the waters" at several waterfront spas and to apply the local mud, which is said to have curative properties. The region is known also for its sparkling wine made from local grapes.

Kherson is a city located at the mouth of the Dnieper River, on the Black Sea between Odessa and Crimea. It has an important shipbuilding industry. Traveling from Odessa to Crimea, one passes near the Askeniya Nova Reserve. It covers an area of about 13,350 acres (33,000 hectares), and preserves steppe grassland that has never been plowed.

Crimea

On the Crimean Peninsula, Simferopol is the regional capital city and is located in the interior. Sevastopol is the naval port that was the target of siege in the Crimean War and is now the base of the Russian fleet. But the coastal city of Yalta may be Crimea's best-known community. Near Yalta is the Nikitsky Botanical Garden, which houses plants from almost every

The Crimean port city of Sevastopol serves as the home of both the Ukrainian Navy's fleet and the Russian Navy's Black Sea fleet. In 1997, Russia and Ukraine signed an agreement in which the Russian fleet was allowed to remain at Sevastopol until 2017.

country in the world. Established in 1812, it has some 28,000 species of plants, including 200 species of roses.

Beaches along the Crimean coast attract vacationers from Ukraine and Russia. Tsar Alexander II built a lavish summer home in Livadia, several miles from Yalta. It was here that the 1945 Yalta Conference, attended by Joseph Stalin, Winston Churchill, and Franklin D. Roosevelt, was held.

Other Russians built more modest vacation homes, called *dachas*, along the coast. Tolstoy vacationed here, as did Chekhov, and it was in Crimea that he wrote two of his best-known plays, *The Cherry Orchard* and *Three Sisters*.

The mountains of Crimea block cold northerly winds and help give the narrow coast strip its mild Mediterranean climate. Geologically, much of Crimea is limestone, the rock type in which caves most often form. The Kara-Dah Nature

Reserve protects some of the region's caves and other unusual rock formations.

The Eastern Region

Kharkov is a large regional cultural center in the northeast. It was founded in the mid-seventeenth century by Cossacks and is now a manufacturing center with factories making tractors, engines, and mining equipment. The factory that previously made T80 tanks now makes equipment for coal mining and sugar refining. The Antonov aircraft factory also is located here.

Donetsk, with a population of more than one million, is a major regional center. It has a university, an array of shops, and is a cultural center with theaters and a philharmonic hall. The area around Krivoy Rog is known for the manufacture of mining machinery, diamond drills, cement, foodstuffs, and timber. The city has a school to train miners and a teacher education center.

Between Kharkov and Kiev is Poltava, site of the 1709 battle in which the Russian tsar, Peter the Great, defeated the Cossacks and their allies, ending their bid to form an independent Cossack state.

The Northern Region

North of Kiev, the grasslands give way to forested land and then, approaching the border with Belarus, to marshlands and wetlands. Chernobyl is in this area, and foreign visitors are comparatively rare. The northwestern region, the Rivne district, is forested. Its mineral resources include basalt and stones for construction materials. The highest elevation in this administrative district, far from the Black Sea, is only 341 feet.

The Chernitov region northeast of Kiev used to be an agricultural area. Its forests were prime sites for gathering mushrooms and wild berries. It is no longer safe to eat these local delicacies. The people now are quite poor, although they continue to raise cattle, pigs, and tobacco.

Following this route through the regions of Ukraine enables a traveler to see and experience the full variety of Ukrainian landscapes, cultural centers, economic activities, and historic influences. It reveals the diversity of a people who now seek to build the country's future as a single nation.

CHAPTER

8

Ukraine Looks Ahead

Ukrainians demonstrated their sense of unity in 1990 with their human chain made up of a half-million people joining hands. As they translate this feeling into patriotism for a new nation, the success of three spheres is pivotal: the government, the economy, and the environment.

Since gaining independence in 1991, Ukraine has taken huge steps toward establishing its presence among the world's nations. For instance, Ukrainians have written and adopted a democratic constitution and held elections within its framework. The government has negotiated several important treaties. The country's boundaries with Russia were secured with the Treaty of Friendship, Cooperation and Partnership, and they have reached agreement with Russia on the use of the naval base at Odessa for the Russian fleet. They have turned over to Russia Soviet nuclear arms that were in the country, and have signed the Nuclear Nonproliferation Treaty. In spite of the country's great need for power, it has closed the nuclear plant at Chernobyl, shutting down the three remaining reactors that remained in operation after the disaster in 1986.

Ukraine has worked with NATO peacekeeping efforts, and has begun discussions with the European Union on the goal of membership. The country also has expressed interest in joining the World Trade Organization. Ukrainians have hosted visits from leaders of the United States, including President Clinton in 1995 and 2000, signifying cooperation and goodwill (and delivery of some much needed foreign aid). Ukraine has cooperated with Russia on launching satellites into space and has a continuing program of Antarctic research.

Since gaining its independence, however, Ukrainians have experienced considerable hardship. Yet, recent economic indicators have shown the economy is improving. Much of the economic growth and development depends on Ukraine having a dependable legal framework. The country has a high literacy rate and a technically trained workforce, both of which are vital to economic success. A very serious issue, however, is the country's declining population. Ukraine, like many other European countries, will need to adopt a practical policy to address the problems resulting from a dwindling population. An adequate labor force is essential to economic growth. Without being self-sufficient in terms of labor, Ukraine's economic reality may remain far behind the developed world for a prolonged period of time. On the other hand, it is well known that many East European countries have experienced a serious "brain drain" since the early 1990s. When unable to prosper at home, educated people tend to leave the country, taking their expertise with them. Ukraine is no exception.

Ukraine's shadow economy, which may represent half of all economic activity, imposes a huge and catastrophic drain on the national treasury, because the goods and services changing hands are not taxed. The shadow economy is also a deterrent to foreign investment. If not checked, failing to comply with legal requirements will become standard. The activities of organized crime must be curbed as well; if the country is to thrive, "Mafia capitalism" must cease to exist.

It is difficult for the government to monitor activities and take appropriate actions when so much economic activity operates outside of legal channels. Another problem is the great swings of boom-and-bust cycles that make the country more vulnerable to external influences. In the mid-1990s, when Russia experienced an economic downturn, the Ukrainian economy suffered severe shock. Ukraine must develop a less fragile economy. The means of achieving this goal are now in hand. They include privatization, foreign investment, and establishing links with the global economy through the WTO and regional economic groups. The current government enthusiastically supports a rapid privatization of the economy.

Businesspeople in the United States look toward Ukraine as a market for products and as a trading partner. Opportunities exist in several areas. Agricultural machinery is in demand and could be manufactured there by foreign investors. (Transporting this heavy equipment can be expensive.) Equipment also is needed to improve airline service and air traffic control systems. As the country's construction business grows, there is a demand for building materials and equipment. Pharmaceuticals and equipment in the medical and dental fields are also needed. Energy companies and power systems need equipment and parts, such as motors, pumps, transformers, fans, turbines, and meters.

The telecommunications industry is in need of modernization, giving rise to demand for fiber optic lines. Demand for modern communications can be expected to increase dramatically. Ukrainian businesses and individuals want extensive and reliable telephone service, as well as e-mail and Internet access, and fax and mobile phone lines.

Tourism also offers many opportunities for investment. Kiev and other major Ukrainian cities are large cosmopolitan

In the years to come, tourism is certain to become an important part of Ukraine's economy. Pictured here are vacationers on a Black Sea beach in the Crimean resort of Yalta.

centers, but they lack hotels with the amenities and services that most Western business travelers desire. The historic architecture and sights, as well as the recreational opportunities of Ukraine's natural landscapes, would attract tourists as well.

North American firms that consider investing in Ukraine can take several approaches. First, they can build plants to manufacture or assemble parts locally. Second, they can enter a joint venture with a Ukrainian partner. Finally, they can send sales representatives to sell their products and take orders, and then ship the items directly to the customer in Ukraine. Each of these, as well as other possible arrangements, has special considerations and consequences. U.S. and Ukrainian license and customs fees vary. The cost of investment, taxes, and duties must be considered, as must possible limits on bringing profits back home to the United States.

As Ukraine pursues economic development, the accompanying social and environmental concerns must be addressed. If agricultural and industrial output is increased at the cost of further atmospheric and water pollution, then it will be a costly trade-off. Developing renewable energy sources would reduce dependence on fossil fuels and could greatly benefit the air quality. Upgrading municipal wastewater treatment plants would reduce the human waste that flows into the rivers. Careful application of agricultural chemicals would reduce the toxic runoff from fields that flows into the waterways.

Some projects would require great investment, such as care for the land around Chernobyl and the people harmed by the fallout, its cleanup, and the continuing exposure to radioactive particles. Some environmental issues require cooperation with neighboring countries. And Ukraine's own people must be educated about the many benefits of protecting the environment from harm.

People of differing backgrounds across the country can be expected to continue to press for recognition and special rights. For example, the Tatars were harshly treated in their expulsion from Crimea by the Soviets. As they return, they expect special help as they reestablish their homes. Also, their demands for either independence or incorporation as a part of Russia have not been realized.

Because of its long-standing link with Russia, Crimea has special standing as an autonomous republic within Ukraine. Eastern Ukraine also has strong economic and cultural links with Russia (as is indicated by their dominant use of the Russian language). But the political influence of this region's people who seek economic integration with Russia should decline as Ukraine's economy strengthens and trade ties are established with other nations.

Features of Ukraine's physical landscape—the steppe grasslands, the many large rivers, the rich soil, and the wealth of natural resources—have been important natural assets to the region's people throughout history. The periods of formal nationhood have been comparatively rare and short-lived in recent centuries, but a new opportunity came with independence in 1991. Ukrainians will shape their future with their own resolve and the support of other countries, both neighbors and more distant states. They face a great challenge of building a modern, market-driven economy. This must be pursued while they work to reduce causes of pollution and clean up past environmental damage. But this is not the first time in their history that the people of Ukraine have met challenges. In looking to the future, they can draw on many proud traditions and proven strengths.

Physical Geography

Location Eastern Europe, bordering the Black Sea, between Poland, Romania, and Moldova in the west and Russia in the east

Area Total: 233,094 square miles (603,700 square kilometers)—slightly smaller than the state of Texas

Climate and Ecosystem Temperate continental; Mediterranean only on the southern Crimean coast; precipitation disproportionately distributed, highest in west and north, lesser in east and southeast; winters vary from cool along the Black Sea to cold farther inland; summers are warm across the greater part of the country, hot in the south

Terrain Most of country consists of fertile plains (steppes) and plateaus, mountains are found only in the west (the Carpathians), and in extreme south, in the Crimean Peninsula

Elevation Extremes Lowest point is Black Sea, sea level; highest point is Hora Hoverla, 6,762 feet (2,061 meters)

Land Use Arable land, 53.8%; permanent crops, 1.5%; other, 44.7% (2005)

Irrigated Land 8,525 square miles (22,080 square kilometers) (2003)

Natural Hazards Flooding; droughts

Environmental Issues Inadequate supplies of potable water; air and water pollution; deforestation; radiation contamination in the northeastern part of the country from the 1986 accident at Chernobyl Nuclear Power Plant

People

Population 46,710,816 (July 2006 est.); males, 21,573,517 (2006 est.); females, 25,137,299 (July 2006 est.)

Population Density 77 people per square kilometer

Population Growth Rate -0.6% (2006 est.)

Net Migration Rate -0.43 migrant(s)/1,000 population (2006 est.)

Fertility Rate 1.17 children born/woman (2006 est.)

Life Expectancy at Birth Total population: 69.98 years; male, 64.71 years; female, 75.59 years (2006 est.)

Median Age Total Population: 39.2 years; male, 35.9 years; female, 42.2 years

Ethnic Groups	Ukrainian, 77.8%; Russian, 17.3%; Belarusian, 0.6%; Moldovan, 0.5%; Crimean Tatar, 0.5%; Bulgarian, 0.4%; Hungarian, 0.3%; Romanian, 0.3%; Polish, 0.3%; Jewish, 0.2%; other, 1.8% (2001 census)
Religions	Ukrainian Orthodox–Kiev Patriarchate, 19%; Orthodox (no particular jurisdiction), 16%; Ukrainian Orthodox–Moscow Patriarchate, 9%; Ukrainian Greek Catholic, 6%; Ukrainian Autocephalous Orthodox, 1.7%; Protestant, Jewish, none, 38% (2004 est.)
Literacy	(age 15 and over can read and write) Total population: 99.7%; male, 99.8%; female, 99.6% (1999 est.)

Economy

Currency	Hryvnia (UAH)
GDP Purchasing Power Parity (PPP)	$319.4 billion (2005 est.)
GDP Per Capita (PPP)	$6,800 (2005 est.)
Labor Force	22.67 million (2005 est.)
Unemployment	2.9% officially registered; large number of unregistered or underemployed workers; the International Labor Organization calculates that Ukraine's real unemployment level is around 9 to 10% (2005 est.)
Labor Force by Occupation	Agriculture, 24%; industry, 32%; services, 44% (1996 est.)
Industries	Coal, electric power, ferrous and nonferrous metals, machinery and transport equipment, chemicals, food processing (especially sugar)
Exports	$38.22 billion (2005 est.)
Imports	$37.18 billion (2005 est.)
Leading Trade Partners	*Exports*: Russia, 18%; Germany, 5.8%; Turkey, 5.7%; Italy, 5%; U.S., 4.6% (2004); *Imports*: Russia, 41.8%; Germany, 9.6%; Turkmenistan, 6.7% (2004)
Export Commodities	Ferrous and nonferrous metals, fuel and petroleum products, chemicals, machinery and transport equipment, food products
Import Commodities	Energy, machinery and equipment, chemicals
Transportation	*Roadways*: total, 105,476 miles (169,739 kilometers); paved, 102,301 miles (164,630 kilometers); unpaved, 3,175 miles (5,109 kilometers) (2003); *Airports:* 537–199 paved (2005); *Railways*: 13,965 miles (22,473

kilometers); *Waterways:* 1,039 miles (1,672 kilometers)—chiefly on the Dnieper River (2006)

Government

Country Name	Conventional long form: none; Conventional short form: Ukraine; Local long form: none; Local short form: Ukrayina; Former: Ukrainian National Republic, Ukrainian State, Ukrainian Soviet Socialist Republic
Capital City	Kiev (Kyiv)
Type of Government	Republic
Head of Government	Prime Minister Yuriy Yekhanurov (since September 22, 2005)
Chief of State	President Viktor A. Yushchenko (since January 23, 2005)
Independence	August 24, 1991 (from the Soviet Union)
Administrative Divisions	24 provinces (oblasti, singular—oblast')

Communications

TV Stations	At least 33 (plus 21 repeaters that relay broadcasts from Russia) (1997)
Phones	(including cellular): 25,877,000 million (2004)
Internet Users	5,278,100 (2005)

* Source: *CIA-The World Factbook* (2006)

History at a Glance

700–400 B.C.	Scythian civilization flourishes.
5th century A.D.	Kiev founded, according to legend and archaeological evidence; Kyi, two brothers and sister, establish Kiev on Dnieper River.
500–600	Slavic peoples migrate into Ukraine.
882	Oleg wins control of Kiev, marking the beginning of Kievan Rus period.
988	Valdimir (Vlodymyr) the Great adopts Christianity for himself and the people of Kievan Rus.
1017–1031	Saint Sophia Cathedral is constructed in Kiev.
1240	Batu Khan leads Mongols in the conquest of Kiev.
1569	Lithuania and Poland unite, and Kiev comes under Polish rule.
1596	Most Ukrainian Orthodox bishops accept Catholicism, and Greek Catholic Church begins; Union of Brest.
1615	Kiev-Mohyla Akademy founded–first Ukrainian institution of higher learning.
1648	Cossack hetman Bohdan Khmelnytsky defeats Poland at Battle of Pyliavtsi.
1654	Khmelnytsky pledges loyalty to Russian tsar in exchange for military aid.
1667	Treaty of Ardrusovo formally partitions Ukraine between Poland and Muscovy (Russia), roughly along the Dnieper River.
1709	Russia defeats Cossacks and their allies at Battle of Poltava.
1772–1795	Partitioning of Poland, whereby much of western Ukraine is transferred to Russia.
1775	Russian army of Catherine the Great destroys remaining Cossacks.
1783	Russia annexes Crimea.
1854	Crimean War breaks out between Russia on one side and Ottoman Empire, Great Britain, and France on the other; Florence Nightingale nurses British soldiers in Crimea.
1856	Treaty of Paris marks end of Crimean War.
1918	Ukrainian National Republic founded.
1921	Treaty of Riga signed, providing for transfer of parts of western Ukraine to Poland, Romania, Czechoslovakia, and the majority of land to Russia.

1922	Ukrainian Soviet Socialist Republic is incorporated into the Union of Soviet Socialist Republics (USSR).
1932–1933	Ukrainians suffer devastating famine resulting from the policies of Joseph Stalin.
1939	Molotov-Ribbentrop pact between Russia and Germany signed, providing for mutual nonaggression and noninterference with internal politics and military; Soviet Red Army advances into Polish Ukraine.
1941	German Army attacks Russian Ukraine.
1941–1944	Nazi Germany occupies Ukraine; Stalin forces Tatars to leave their homes in Crimea.
1945	Franklin D. Roosevelt, Winston Churchill, and Joseph Stalin meet in Yalta and decide how Allies will administer European countries after World War II; Ukraine joins United Nations as a charter (original) member.
1954	Soviet premier Nikita Khrushchev transfers Crimea to Ukraine in commemorating 300th anniversary of Russian–Ukrainian union.
1986	Reactor at Chernobyl nuclear power plant explodes.
1986–89	Soviet premier Mikhail Gorbachev establishes *perestroika* and *glasnost*.
1989	Rukh independence movement founded.
1991	In August, Ukrainian parliament declares independence from USSR; in December, Ukrainians vote overwhelmingly for independence.
1994	Ukraine, Russia, and United States sign agreement calling for Ukrainian nuclear disarmament; Leonid Kuchma elected president of Ukraine.
1996	New currency, *hryvnia*, introduced.
1997	Treaty of Friendship signed by Russia and Ukraine (ratified in 1999); Russia renounces claims on Crimea; Ukraine agrees that Russian fleet can remain at Sevastopol for 20 years.
1998	Ukrainian Communist Party wins approximately one-fourth of seats in *Rada* (parliament); currency (hryvnia) devalued by 51 percent.
1999	Kuchma elected to second five-year term.
2000	Chernobyl nuclear power plant shut down.
2002	In parliamentary elections, party of the president wins 23 percent of vote; opposition party of Viktor Yushchenko wins 25 percent; Communist Party wins 15 percent.
2004	Viktor Yushchenko wins presidential election.

Glossary

alluvium: collection of silt, clay, and similar material carried by a flowing river and deposited as sediment.

Bolsheviks: Violent Russian revolutionaries, responsible for overthrowing Russian tsar in 1917 and establishing Communist Party.

borscht: Ukrainian soup made with beets, other vegetables, and meat; often topped with sour cream.

Chernozem: A rich, fertile soil found in much of Ukrainian steppe grasslands; a type of mollisol.

CIS: Commonwealth of Independent States; organization of 11 former Soviet republics.

dacha: Country retreat.

glasnost: Political openness. Policy instituted in mid-1980s by Soviet premier Mikhail Gorbachev.

hetman: Elected Cossack chieftain, leader.

Hetmanate: Government under a hetman.

hryvnia: Unit of Ukrainian currency.

Khazars: People of empire based at mouth of Volga River; traders with Kievan Rus in eighth and ninth centuries.

mollisol: A type of soil, rich in organic matter and important for agriculture.

oblast: Regional administrative unit, comparable to a state or province.

oligarch: One of very few people who are politically or economically powerful.

perestroika: Restructuring; refers primarily to Soviet economic policy of late 1980s characterized by less central control of industry and agriculture.

pysanka: Ukrainian Easter egg.

Rada: Ukrainian parliament; also called Supreme Council.

Rukh: People's Front of Ukraine for Reconstruction, founded in 1989; became a movement for independence; after 1991, a political party.

Scythian: Civilization in Ukraine, circa 700 B.C. to 400 B.C.

serf: Peasant who worked the land under the control of the landowner; essentially a slave.

Slav: Ethnic peoples, originally from Central Asia, who migrated to Russia, Eastern Europe, Ukraine.

steppe: Vast area of level or gently rolling land, typically naturally covered in grasses.

Tatars: Mongols, Muslims who settled in Crimea.

Trypillian: Early documented culture in Ukraine, approximately 4000 B.C.–2000 B.C.

tsar: Title of Russian rulers before 1917.

Uniate Church: Christian faith utilizing Orthodox forms of worship while acknowledging leadership of Roman Catholic pope.

Varangians: A branch of Vikings from Scandinavia who established Kievan Rus society in Ukraine in ninth century; also known as Rus.

Names

Traditional (Russian) Spelling	Ukrainian Spelling
Chernobyl	Chornobyl
Dnepropetrovsk	Dnipropetrovsk
Dnieper River	Dnipro River
Dniester River	Dnister River
Donets'k	Donetske
Kharkov	Kharkiv
Kiev	Kyiv
Krivoy Rog	Kryvy Rih
Odessa	Odesa

Bibliography

Allen, W. *The Ukraine: A History.* New York: Russell and Russell, Inc., 1963.

D'Anieri, Paul J., Robert Kravchuk, and Taras Kuzio *Politics and Society in Ukraine.* Boulder, Colo.: Westview Press, 1999.

Fisher, Alan W. *The Crimean Tatars.* Stanford, Calif.: Hoover Institution Press, 1978.

Hamm, Michael F. *Kiev: A Portrait.* Princeton, N.J.: Princeton University Press, 1993.

Kubijovyc, Volodymyr. *Ukraine: A Concise Encyclopedia.* Toronto: University of Toronto Press, 1963.

Manning, Clarence A. *Twentieth-Century Ukraine.* New York: Bookman Associates, 1995.

———. *The Story of the Ukraine.* New York: Philosophical Library, 1947.

Subtelny, Orest. *Ukraine: A History.* Toronto: University of Toronto Press, 2000.

Tismaeanu, Vladimir. *Political Culture and Civil Society in Russia and the New States of Eurasia.* New York: M.E. Sharpe, Inc., 1995.

Web sites

Crimean Tatars Page
http://www.euronet.nl/users/sota/krimtatar.html

Ukraine Government Home Page
http://www.kmu.gov.ua/control/

Online Translation Dictionary
http://lingresua.tripod.com/online/

The World Factbook
http://www.cia.gov/cia/publications/factbook/docs/faqs.html

U.S. Department of State Background Note on Ukraine
http://www.state.gov/r/pa/ei/bgn/3211.htm

D'Avignon, Tania. *Simply Ukraine*. Atrex Management, 1998.

Magocsi, Paul Robert. *A History of Ukraine*. Seattle, Wash.: University of Washington Press, 1996.

Reid, Anna, *Borderland: A Journey through the History of Ukraine*. Boulder, Colo.: Westview Press, 1999.

Shcherbak, Iurii. *Chernobyl: A Documentary Story*. Edmonton, Alberta: Canadian Institute of Ukrainian Study, 1989.

Wilson, Andrew. *The Ukrainians: Unexpected Nation*. New Haven, Conn.: Yale University Press, 2002.

Web sites

The Chernobyl Disaster
http://www.chernobyl.info/

CIA World Factbook Site on Ukraine
http://www.cia.gov/cia/publications/factbook/geos/up.html

Encyclopedia of Ukraine
http://www.encyclopediaofukraine.com/

Kievan Rus
http://www.mnsu.edu/emuseum/history/russia/kievanrus.html

Welcome to Ukraine
http://www.wumag.kiev.ua/index2.php?param=anews

Index

Index

Index

About the Contributors

CATHERINE W. COOPER earned a Master of Arts degree in geography at the George Washington University, where she was a research fellow with the Institute for Urban Environmental Research. Cooper formerly worked as an adjunct professor in the Geography Department at George Washington and currently works for the Eastern Shore Land Conservancy.

ZORAN "ZOK" PAVLOVIĆ is a cultural geographer currently working at Oklahoma State University in Stillwater. *Ukraine* is the eighth book Pavlović authored or coauthored for the Chelsea House geography book series MODERN WORLD NATIONS. He also authored *Europe* for the MODERN WORLD CULTURES series. In geography his interests are culture theory, evolution of geographic thought, and geography of viticulture. He was born and raised in southeastern Europe.

Series Editor **CHARLES F. GRITZNER** is distinguished professor of geography at South Dakota State University in Brookings. He is now in his fifth decade of college teaching, research, and writing. In addition to teaching, he enjoys writing, working with teachers, and sharing his love of geography with readers. As the series editor for Chelsea House's MODERN WORLD CULTURES and MODERN WORLD NATIONS series, he has a wonderful opportunity to combine each of these hobbies. Gritzner has served as both president and executive director of the National Council for Geographic Education and has received the Council's highest honor, the George J. Miller Award for Distinguished Service to Geographic Education.

Picture Credits